LAWNS

LAWNS

The year-round lawn-care handbook
for all climates and conditions,
plus a special section on ground covers

MELVIN J. ROBEY

David McKay Company, Inc.

NEW YORK

Library of Congress Cataloging in Publication Data

Robey, Melvin J
    Lawns.

    Includes index.
      1. Lawns. 2. Ground cover plants. I. Title.
SB433.R55   635.9′64   77–23012
ISBN 0–679–50665–9

10 9 8 7 6 5 4 3 2 1

MANUFACTURED IN THE UNITED STATES OF AMERICA

Contents

Preface

Have you ever had a question on how to perform a lawn-care chore but couldn't find the answer to it? You probably spent hours thumbing through various references but were unable to put your finger on the answer to your problem. This book will solve this dilemma for you.

You'll find the lawn-care techniques used by the experts presented in an easy-to-understand, down-to-earth question-and-answer style. This approach to solving those nagging lawn-care problems will prove invaluable to you. You can quickly scan through the questions until you find the ones related to your particular needs. This eliminates the need for reading entire chapters just to find answers to those pesty questions.

Once you have found the solution to your particular problems there is a year-round lawn-care guide to help you in your general planning. No longer will you have to guess about weed control, fertilizing, seeding, and the other lawn-care chores. This handy reference takes the worry out of yard work and allows you to develop a luxurious lawn with a minimum of effort. If you follow the month-by-month guide to lawn care, you will prevent minor problems from becoming major disasters.

Why not surprise your friends with your landscaping skills by using ground cover plants to beautify your property? Strategically placed ground cover beds will add a touch of elegance to your outdoor surroundings. Be sure to consult the section on plants suitable to your region when landscaping your lawn. A map will show you which plants are adapted for use in your area. Specialized categories are also listed so you can select plants to meet your specific needs.

Seventy percent of all pesticide-related deaths occur to children 5 years old or younger. If this statistic startles you then be sure to read the special introduction to the chapter on insects and their control. Above all, you will want to keep pesticides away from your children.

Whether your goal is to have the most attractive lawn in the neighborhood or just to grow healthy grass and keep the weeds out, this book is designed to help you. There are numerous illustrations and tables which will enable you to better understand the answers more fully and for your quick reference. You will also find the glossary helpful for those words or phrases unfamiliar to you.

As you read through the chapters, remember to mark those questions and answers which are uppermost in your mind. This will help you quickly locate them when you are ready to try a new technique or to solve a lawn-care problem.

Good luck with your lawn!

MELVIN J. ROBEY

1

You and Your Lawn

A LUXURIOUS LAWN WILL EMPHASIZE
THE BEAUTY OF YOUR HOME

Every year millions of homeowners ask the same questions about their lawns. In most instances the books available to them are miniature encyclopedias that are very confusing and discouraging to the reader. Often it takes hours to find the answers to their problems.

In writing this book I brought together the basic principles and agronomic techniques used in lawn care, and I put this information in an easy-to-read question-and-answer style to help the homeowner understand how to develop a healthy, beautiful lawn. The result is a book you can just flip open to the chapter related to your problems and quickly scan the questions until you find those concerning your particular problems. The rest of the questions and their answers can be skipped over and read when you have more time to explore the secrets of having a beautiful lawn. By not having to read the entire book, you can spend as little as five to ten minutes finding the solution to your lawn problems.

Why not keep this book near your favorite chair, where you can spend a few minutes thumbing through the chapters of interest to you? As you do, remember to mark those questions and answers that are uppermost in your mind. This will help you find them quickly when you are ready to try a new lawn-care technique.

Modern times have turned your lawn into an outdoor living area, which means it needs tender loving care to be developed into a beautiful, living carpet for your outdoor pleasure. A rich, dark-green, cushiony turf can reach the peak of perfection when it has the best care. You can develop a luxurious lawn without being a lawn-care expert. An attractive lawn can easily be yours if you understand how to manage your lawn-care program and then do everything at the correct time throughout the year.

A NICE LAWN ADDS TO THE VALUE OF YOUR HOME

How much do you think a well-groomed lawn is worth? Your answer to this question will vary, depending on your use of the lawn and your future plans for it. If you are planning on selling your home, then the appearance of your lawn becomes very important. As a rule, a nice lawn will increase the overall value of your property. Prospective buyers form a first impression of your home by the exterior, and this, of course, includes the lawn. If the lawn is unsightly and weed infested, selling the house will take longer than if your lawn is well kept and looks like a green velvety carpet. Often potential buyers will not even bother to look at a house if the outside appearance is unattractive. And, unfortunately, this can also be the case if you have a nice lawn but several neighbors around you have poorly maintained lawns.

Homeowners frequently would like a monetary value placed on their lawns, but it is difficult to attach a cash value to a living plant such as grass. Estimates I have read show a healthy, thick, luxurious lawn is worth 2 to 4 percent of the sales value of your home. If your house is worth $28,000, then your lawn value is between $560 and $1,120 (assuming it is in good shape).

But the real value of a nice lawn should be found not in the monetary value but rather in the pleasure you obtain from it with your family or your friends, whether it be for a barbecue or a game of badminton. How often have you dropped down in your patio chair in the evening after a hard day and reflected back on the day's events? A few relaxing minutes spent in the pleasant atmosphere of your outdoor surroundings at home can be very refreshing and can make the evening's chores more enjoyable.

Think of your lawn as a picture frame. Selecting the wrong frame for a painting can ruin its appearance: the same principle applies to your house and your lawn. A poor, weed-infested, yellowish, underfed lawn is very uncomplimentary to your home. Your lawn should do for your house what a well-selected picture frame does for an exquisite painting. Both should compliment the subjects they are encompassing, and both should accentuate their beauty.

HOMEOWNERS AND THEIR LAWNS

If you were to spend a few weeks talking with homeowners about their lawns, you would soon discover that homeowners can be divided into three distinct groups: the eager novice, the experienced lawnskeeper, and the lawn enthusiast. There are, of course, many cases where the homeowners' attitudes toward their lawn place them in two or more of these groups.

Let's take a quick glance at the individuals in the various groups and see where you fit. The term *eager novice* would usually apply to newlyweds living in their first home, or to someone who has just bought a new house. Usually these novices are young, and they attach much importance to the image they are presenting to neighbors and friends. They have been told that a beautiful, luxurious lawn will increase the value of their home, and they are therefore willing to spend the time and money on their lawn to protect their overall investment. In these first years of learning about lawns and their care, homeowners will buy many different products at random before they settle down to one or two brand names and follow their recommendations. It is at this point that the eager novices step into one of the two remaining groups.

If the step is into the experienced lawnskeeper group, then you can expect to see them spending less time on their lawns and enjoying them more. Those who fit into this group have spent several years experimenting with various lawn products and have met with success and failure in their attempts to have a luxurious lawn. They have used just about everything on the market and have concluded that none of the materials fully lives up to its claims.

What these homeowners really feel about lawn care is that it is something they are forced to do when they would rather be golfing, shopping, reading, or just loafing around the house. If given a set of easy-to-understand rules on how to take care of their lawns, they will follow them, provided a lot of hard, tedious work is not involved. These homeowners are not interested in becoming lawn-care experts, but they do realize the social pressures of producing at least a decent-looking lawn to keep the neighbors happy. If you were to meet some of these people at a party and the topic of lawn care were brought up, they would usually give you a blow-by-blow description of why your lawn is doing so poorly. A quick check of their lawn the next day would help you realize that you're not the only person in town who would rather use spare time for golfing or shopping.

The other category the eager novice can step into after years of hard work and preparation is that of the lawn enthusiast. Every neighborhood has at least one person who falls into this group, and usually this person has the nicest lawn. Members of this group are labeled lawn enthusiasts, Green Thumb, or lawn fanatics. Everyone envies the success this group has in developing a velvety-green lawn. These people are usually well established in the community and have an income that allows them to be a little more particular in the maintenance of their lawns. A pleasant evening to them is working in the yard, enjoying the exercise and fresh air. After dark you will often find them curled up in a favorite chair, refreshment at hand, reading a garden catalogue or planning on when the next bag of fertilizer should be applied.

In discussing the different attitudes toward lawns, I have exaggerated some of the traits that occur in homeowners and their techniques in caring for their lawns. Almost everyone of us fits into each of the groups at various times during the years. Quite often we use the lawn as an excuse to get out of doing less enjoyable tasks.

GRASS AND THE ENVIRONMENT

A homeowner's first thoughts about grass may bring on visions of a lawn where the children are able to romp and play. The farmer thinks about the important role grass plays in making his pasture land topnotch. Seldom do we give a second thought to how the grass plant might otherwise affect the world in which we live.

With today's concern about environmental issues, it is nice to know that the plant kingdom is doing its share. This is especially true of the grass family.

Just how does a grass plant help the environment? You'll be

surprised as you read of the unique benefits that grass has to offer.

Air Purification

The green leaves of grass absorb, from the air, carbon dioxide, emitted by cars and factories, and sulfur dioxide, and convert them into pure oxygen. This is a natural purification process that occurs daily. An average-size lawn can easily release enough oxygen for a family of four each day.

Heat Reduction

Turf grasses and other plants act as a natural air conditioner by helping to control temperatures through transpiration; that is, evaporation of water from plant leaves. Lawn grasses will cause the temperature at ground level to be 20 to 30 degrees cooler than at adjacent paved areas.

Noise Control

Grasses, as well as shrubs, trees, and other ornamentals, will reduce undesirable noise levels by 20 to 30 percent. The deflection, absorption, and reduction of traffic and community sounds are bound to improve your living conditions.

Erosion Prevention

A healthy turf can absorb large quantities of water and can reduce runoffs, which can carry soil particles, debris, and chemicals into nearby streams, lakes, and reservoirs. A soil bank, regardless of the amount of slope, is more susceptible to erosion if it is bare than if it has a good sod cover.

Supports Wildlife

Grass serves as a natural source of food for the numerous animals found on the lawns of millions of homeowners. For example, birds find a wide variety of seeds and insects to feast upon among the grass blades.

Natural Filter

The fine dust particles floating around in the air are trapped among the grass blades, eventually getting mixed in with the soil.

This natural cleaning of the air makes life more enjoyable for millions of people every day.

LAWN CARE AND THE ENERGY CRISIS

How are lawn care and the energy crisis related? Many of the products used in maintaining a lawn are made from oil or oil by-products. Probably the best example that really shows the impact of lawn care on oil consumption is the use of gasoline in lawn mowers.

Let's assume the average homeowner mowing once a week uses at least 7 gallons of gasoline a year to keep his lawn looking nice. Now suppose 40 million homowners use this same amount of gasoline for upkeep of their lawns. By simple mathematics you can readily see that 280 million gallons of gasoline are used each year. Although this may seem like a tremendous amount of gasoline, don't be too quick to advocate giving this up as a means of conserving fuel. You could return to the manual push mower, but the overall effect would be rather insignificant. If you really want to conserve gasoline, the best way to do it is to observe the 55-mile-per-hour speed limit. If everyone would drive this limit, 7 to 9 billion gallons of gasoline would be saved in a year.

Another area where lawn care and the energy crisis cross paths is in the use of pesticides (weed, disease, and insect killers); most are manufactured from petroleum. Discontinuing the use of pesticides just because they are made from oil is not justifiable. However, using them discreetly, with good judgment and with a little sense, will help accomplish the chore of controlling the pests around your yard, while reducing the amount of oil-based chemicals used. In this way you will be helping to protect our environment by decreasing chemical pollution.

SCHEDULING OF LAWN CARE IMPORTANT

When you are planning on spending all day Saturday working outside, you want the satisfaction of accomplishing your goals. Your time is valuable, and you prefer not to waste any of it in the yard or anywhere else, for that matter. This also holds true for the money you have invested in fertilizer, seed, weed-killers, and any other lawn-care products you bought at the garden center. To be sure that the time and money you are investing in your lawn on Saturday will return the dividends you expect, you should have an understanding of the plants you are working with and their needs. Grass plants have their own particular wants and desires and therefore do better when fed, mowed, watered, and debugged at specific times of the year.

As you read through the chapters of this book, becoming acquainted with grass, you will acquire an understanding for the need to follow Mother Nature's own time-table for doing things. The proper scheduling of the different lawn-care techniques is really one of the keys to having a beautiful lawn.

In Chapter 11 you will find a month-by-month guide for achieving a beautiful lawn. You will notice that each month's discussion is separated into two regions, North and South. Check the map at the beginning of Chapter 2 (p. 10) to determine which region you are living in. Thereafter you can follow either the North or South guide for maintaining your lawn and keeping in tune with nature. Following the month-by-month discussion and supplementing it with the information found in the other chapters will help you in your lawn-care endeavors. Add to this your own common knowledge of what works best for your lawn and you have the formula for developing an elegant lawn.

2

Grasses for Home Lawns

1. What is meant by the terms warm-climate and cool-climate grasses?

The United States can be roughly divided into five separate regions, according to the different climatic conditions. (See map on p. 10.) The Northern regions (1, 2, and 3) are most suitable for cool-climate grasses, and the Southern regions (4 and 5) more desirable for warm-climate grasses.

2. What are some of the warm-climate and cool-climate grasses?

Warm Climate	Cool Climate
Bermudagrass	Bentgrass
Carpetgrass	Kentucky bluegrass
Centipedegrass	Tall Fescue
St. Augustinegrass	Red Fescue
Zoysia	*Poa trivialis* (rough bluegrass)

3. There are so many different kinds of grasses to choose from. Which is the best to buy?

The homeowner is usually restricted to what is available at the lawn and garden centers. Read the seed labels carefully to find out what is in the bag or box and compare the grass varieties with what you have learned in this book, especially the information in this chapter.

Which Kentucky Bluegrass Fits Your Needs?

There are more than 20 species of Kentucky bluegrass from which you can choose. Many of the newer varieties are low-grow-

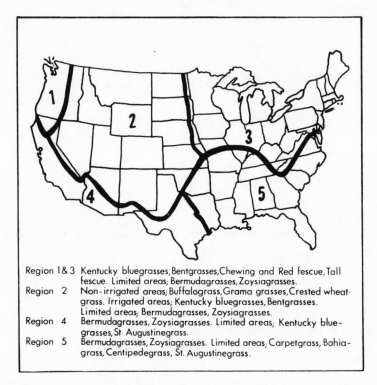

Region 1& 3   Kentucky bluegrasses, Bentgrasses, Chewing and Red fescue, Tall fescue. Limited areas; Bermudagrasses, Zoysiagrasses.

Region 2   Non-irrigated areas; Buffalograss, Grama grasses, Crested wheatgrass. Irrigated areas; Kentucky bluegrasses, Bentgrasses. Limited areas; Bermudagrasses, Zoysiagrasses.

Region 4   Bermudagrasses, Zoysiagrasses. Limited areas; Kentucky bluegrasses, St. Augustinegrass.

Region 5   Bermudagrasses, Zoysiagrasses. Limited areas; Carpetgrass, Bahiagrass, Centipedegrass, St. Augustinegrass.

Regions where turfgrasses are best suited for home-lawn use.

ing (dwarf) grasses that can be mowed for a neater, more uniform-looking lawn. They have excellent disease-resistance, but they require more care and cost considerably more than the older varieties. If you are putting in a new lawn or renovating an old one, consider the newer varieties.

Looking over the following list will allow you to quickly pick out the bluegrasses that fit your needs.

Ordinary Kentucky Bluegrasses. Any variety of bluegrass that has similar characteristics to, or has been only slightly improved from, those of common Kentucky bluegrass. They were developed primarily for home-lawn use and, because of their upright growth and disease susceptibility, they are not among the better varieties to use in a well-groomed lawn.

EXAMPLES: Arboretum, Campus, Delft, Kenblue, Newport, Nu-Dwarf, Park, and Troy.

Improved Kentucky Bluegrasses. Many of the bluegrasses in this category are excellent for home-lawn use but are still not the top of the line in bluegrass varieties. They have good disease-resistance and produce seed easily. This helps to hold down the price of seed, so many homeowners readily use them.

EXAMPLES: Arista, Baron, Cougar, Prato, Sydsport, Vista, and Windsor.

Elite Kentucky Bluegrasses. These bluegrasses are for the home-owners who want a first-class lawn. The grasses in this group respond exceptionally well to good management and can be mowed at three fourths of an inch to give you a professional-looking lawn. The elite bluegrasses are for the enthusiastic owners who want a grass that will respond to their tender loving care. Even with a minimum of care these grasses will give you as good a lawn as the ordinary and improved varieties.

EXAMPLES: Adelphi, Bonnieblue, Fylking (0217), Merion, Nugget, Pennstar, Sodco, Warren's A-20, Warren's A-34, Glade, and Galaxy.

Bermudagrass Varieties, (not for Northern states)

FLORATURF   Excellent for home lawns, has some shade tolerance; disease and insect problems can occur. (Released by Florida AES*.)

MIDWAY   Produces a medium-textured lawn, good cold tolerance, probably does best in the northern parts of the Southern grass region. (Released by Kansas AES.)

ORMOND   Vigorous grower, poor cold tolerance, therefore restricted to southern portions of the Southern grass region. (Developed by Florida AES.)

ROYAL CAPE   Extreme heat and salt tolerance, good desert-area grass. (Developed in California.)

SANTA ANA   Withstands heavy wear, good for play areas, poor cold tolerance, exhibits tolerance to smoke and automobile fumes. (Released by California AES.)

* Agricultural Experimental Station

SUNTURF   Good color and spreads rapidly. (Developed by several different state colleges.)

TIFDWARF   A dwarf variety that tolerates very close mowing (three sixteenths of an inch), most commonly used for golf greens. (Released from Tifton, Georgia.)

TIFFINE   Good disease tolerance, medium-textured leaves, excellent for a well-manicured lawn. (Released from Tifton, Georgia.)

TIFGREEN   Good disease tolerance, nice green color when fertilized, one of the best varieties for home lawns if well cared for. (Released from Tifton, Georgia.)

TIFLAWN   A rugged, wear-resistant variety that gets by on small amounts of fertilizer, shows good resistance to disease and frost, spreads quickly to form a uniform turf. (Released from Tifton, Georgia.)

TIFWAY   Another good home-lawn variety, excellent disease resistance and good color for a lawn grass. (Released from Tifton, Georgia.)

U-3   Some tolerance to cool weather, is adapted to most of the Southern grass regions. (Developed by USGA* Green Section.)

4. At what temperatures do the grasses grow best?

Northern grass varieties do best in mild temperatures ranging from 60 to 80 degrees. (See p. 201 for Celsius figures.) When the temperature is higher than 80 degrees, the grass uses up its food supply too rapidly and then goes dormant; that is, it stops growing and turns brown. Growth resumes when temperatures cool down, provided adequate moisture is available.

The Southern grasses grow best whenever the temperatures are above 70 to 75 degrees. Whenever the temperature drops below 50 degrees, many of the Southern grasses will start to turn brown and go into dormancy until the next warm spell. (See fig. 2–1.)

5. What exactly is the difference between an annual and a perennial grass?

An annual grass, such as some varieties of ryegrass, completes its entire life cycle in a one-year period. This means it develops from seed early in the year and then produces seed at the end of the growing season before it dies.

* United States Golf Association

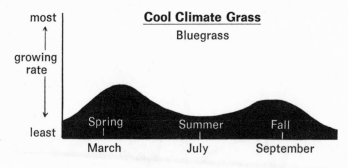

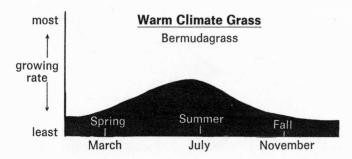

Figure 2–1. Seasonal growing habits of two turfgrasses.

A perennial grass is one that survives season after season, producing seed every year. These grasses are the preferred ones for home lawns. Bluegrass, Bermudagrass, and zoysia are examples of perennial grasses.

6. What is the difference between a rhizome and a stolon?

A rhizome is an underground stem that grows out from the grass plant and sends up new plants. A stolon grows above the ground along the surface, and new plants develop from it. (See fig. 2–2.)

7. What is meant by the term tillering?

Tillers are new plants that develop from the base of the parent plant and help to make a lawn thicker and more uniform. Almost every grass will produce tillers, whether they are the bunch or the spreading variety.

8. Why doesn't grass stop growing when it is cut off as does a limb or twig on a tree?

Without getting too technical, it's a matter of where the new growth is produced in the plants. Trees, shrubs, and evergreens have terminal buds (points where new growth is initiated) that

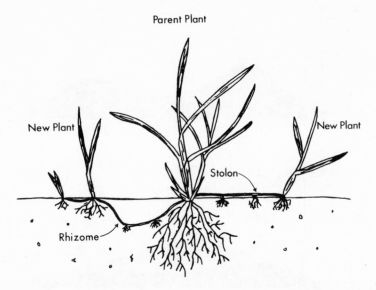

Figure 2–2. Offshoots of parent plant grow from either the rhizome or the stolon.

are located at the tips of the limbs and twigs. When these buds are removed by pruning, growth is stopped because of the removal of that part of the plant that produces the new growth each year.

In grass, the growing points are located at the base (crown) of the plant, and new growth is produced low to the ground. So, when you cut the grass, you are removing the older portion of the leaves and making room for the younger leaves to push up. Setting a mower too low results in scalping the lawn and removing the growing points of the grass, thus killing it.

9. *I have often heard that a healthy lawn is really important because of the way it helps to improve the condition of the soil. Just what does the grass plant do to improve the soil?*

Grasses have a fibrous root system that spreads throughout the soil in search of water and nutrients. A healthy lawn will produce 50 pounds of roots per 1,000 square feet each year. Almost half of these roots die and are replaced by new ones each year. The old roots decompose and help the soil to become granular and well aerated. When the roots decompose, they leave in the soil millions of minute channels that increase the air pockets in the ground.

The old roots also serve as a source of food for microorganisms responsible for the release of some nutrients in the soil.

10. *I just bought a home that is two years old, and the lawn is terrible. How can I tell what kind of grasses were planted by the contractor who built the house?*

It is difficult for a homeowner to identify lawn grasses without the proper charts. For accurate identification have your county extension agent help you, but you can make this quick test first and perhaps identify the grasses yourself. Check to see if the grass tends to grow in clumps and has wide shiny leaves, and check if the leaf tips are jagged and frayed after each mowing. If the grass fits all these characteristics, then it is probably ryegrass the contractor used to get a quick green lawn after finishing the house.

11. *What do you think of putting a small golf green in my back lawn?*

I think it is an excellent idea if you are an avid golfer with a big back lawn and like to spend your spare time in the evenings and on weekends working outdoors. This is especially true if you use bentgrass or Bermudagrass for the green. Both of these grasses require a very high degree of maintenance when mowed short enough for a putting green. You also need a special reel mower for the cutting of a green to get a good, true putting surface.

If you live in the Northern part of the United States, then I have a suggestion that is somewhat of a compromise. Some of the new bluegrass varieties can be mowed at three quarters of an inch if they have adequate moisture and fertilizer, and if they are on a soil with good drainage. By using a bluegrass for your green, you can use the same chemicals (fertilizers, weed killers, insecticides) on all your lawn, thus reducing the large supply of different chemicals needed to maintain two kinds of grass. A small, hand-pushed reel mower, which can be set to cut at three quarters of an inch, will work very well for this type of green. For putting, a bluegrass green will not serve as well as a good bentgrass or Bermudagrass green, but it should give you a good enough putting surface for your needs.

12. *I just moved to a new state and need to do some work on the front lawn around our new home. Should I use the same grass seed as I did at my old home?*

Maybe. The answer depends on the differences in climate. For example, if you lived in Indianapolis, Indiana, and moved two hundred miles south to Louisville, Kentucky, then the bluegrass that gave you a beautiful lawn in Indianapolis would have a difficult time surviving in the hot, humid weather in the South. One of the best ways to find out what kind of grass to grow is to drive around your neighborhood until you find the nicest lawn. Then stop and find out what kind of grass it is and how the owner makes it look so nice. This will give you some idea of what to look for when you go to the local garden center to buy seed.

13. I just planted a black walnut tree in my back lawn. I've been told that when the tree reaches maturity other shrubs and plants will not grow near it. Is this true?

Certain plants can be killed if their roots come in contact with those of the walnut tree. Death is caused by a chemical released from the roots of the walnut tree. Fortunately this chemical has no ill effects on grass plants and therefore is not a problem. In fact, it stimulates the growth of the grass plant. But the heavy shade, after the tree matures, can cause the grass to become weakened and susceptible to disease.

14. Does it matter what kind of grass I plant in my lawn?

This depends on what you want, a cow pasture or a luxurious lawn. If you select the wrong grass, the best possible care will still produce a poor lawn. An example of this would be trying to grow a sun-loving grass in heavy shade. The type of grass selected will determine how nice a lawn you will have.

15. When selecting a grass variety for a lawn, what facts about the grass must I take into consideration?

First, you must consider the suitability or adaptability of the grass for the kinds of weather in your area. You need to understand the characteristics of the grass so you'll know how it will react under the various conditions to which it will be subjected. You also need to know what type of management it will require once it is established around your home. Selection of the proper grass is basic to having a luxurious lawn of which you can be proud. See Table 2–1 for the basic characteristics of different turfgrasses.

16. What types of grasses will do best in the shade?

Certain types of grasses are more adaptable to shady conditions than others. Red fescue, chewing fescue, *Poa trivialis*, and St. Augustinegrass are four of the more shade-tolerant grasses available. The shade tolerance of most turfgrasses is enhanced the fur-

TABLE 2–1

Characteristics of Different Turfgrasses

	Shade Tolerance	Disease Resistance	Nitrogen Requirements	Winter Hardiness	Drought Resistance
Bentgrass	med.	low	high	high	low
Bermudagrass	low	med.	high	low	high
Kentucky Bluegrass	low	med.	med.	high	med.
Carpetgrass	med.	med.	low	low	low
Centipedegrass	med.	high	low	low	low
Chewing Fescue	high	med.	low	high	med.
Red Fescue	high	med.	low	high	med.
Ryegrass	low	med.	med.	med.	med.
St. Augustine	high	low	med.	low	low
Tall Fescue	med.	high	low	high	high
Zoysia	med.	high	low	med.	high

ther south they are grown. And the bluegrass variety Glade appears to do well in shade.

17. How can I tell if I should plant ground cover instead of trying to grow grass in my yard?

Ground cover should be used any time heavy shade prevents growth of grass, or when extreme heat makes it impossible for grass to do well, or if banks are too steep to mow, or when you want a contrast in the appearance of your lawn areas. (Please see Chapters 12–17, pp. 149–199, for more information on ground covers.)

18. In my lawn are some small patches of grass that have been identified as annual bluegrass, but they don't seem to die each year. If it is an annual, why does it live longer than one year?

Annual bluegrass is considered to be an annual grass but under certain climatic conditions it will survive for more than one year. It is also a prolific seed producer and can easily reseed itself, giving the appearance of being a perennial plant, when in truth it is just developing new plants each year from seeds of the dead plants.

19. Is annual bluegrass a weed or a lawn grass?

In most instances I would consider it a weed rather than a desirable lawn grass. You will find it listed on grass-seed labels as a noxious weed, one you should avoid getting started in your lawn. Its presence usually indicates a lack of good lawn care. This grass is used to overseed into dormant grasses in the Southern regions of the United States, mostly on golf greens. The hot, humid weather in the summer causes it to die and the other grasses to take over.

20. Should clover be seeded along with grass seed in a new lawn?

This depends on the individual and whether there is a preference for clover in a lawn. In the past, clover was used as a way of increasing the nitrogen content of the soil, but it is seldom used in good mixtures today. The staining properties (to children's clothing especially) of the clover plant, along with the undesirable white blossoms, are two reasons why it is usually excluded from lawn-seed mixtures.

21. I have seen two or three differently named ryegrasses used in seed packages. Which ryegrass is best for use on a home lawn?

You must first decide how long you want the ryegrass in your lawn. If you are using it for a quick green-up while the other lawn grasses get established, then be sure to use the annual (Italian) ryegrass. Read the label carefully to be sure no perennial ryegrass seed is in the bag. If the term *domestic ryegrass* is present, then you are getting a mixture of annual and perennial ryegrass. If you want the ryegrass to be present in your lawn, then select a perennial variety.

Today there are several improved varieties that have a finer leaf blade than do the older common varieties. These new varieties make an excellent addition to the available turfgrasses and merit consideration for use in your lawn. Manhattan, NK-100, Norlea, Pelo, NK-200, and Pennfine are a few of the new, improved ryegrass varieties now available, with Manhattan and Pennfine being the best for home-lawn use.

22. I see advertisements about the "miracle grass" zoysia. Is it as good as the advertisements claim it to be?

Zoysia is a good lawn grass if properly managed and grown in the right climate. I do think it has been oversold to the homeowner as the cure-all for lawn problems. Before putting zoysia into a lawn, you had better have a good understanding of its growth habits and maintenance requirements.

23. What are some of the advantages and disadvantages of having a zoysia lawn?

The ability of zoysia to withstand close mowing and heavy wear, its low nitrogen requirements, its resistance to various diseases and to insect problems are some advantages to a zoysia lawn.

The two real disadvantages are its inability to do well in shady areas and the fact that it becomes dormant (turns brown) in the fall in the Northern part of the United States and remains so until late spring. Many people spray their lawns with green dye during this dormant period.

24. How long will it take for my zoysia plugs to fill in and form a thick lawn?

If you use 2-inch to 3-inch plugs and put them in on 12-inch centers throughout your lawn, then I would estimate 2–3 years before your lawn will be totally zoysia. By adding fertilizer during the first two years, you might be able to shorten this time. Controlling weeds while the zoysia is filling in can present a problem. Don't let weeds compete with the zoysia, or you'll be waiting more than 2–3 years for your zoysia to form a thick, resilient turf.

25. Will zoysia crowd out other grasses?

Yes. It will predominate and will spread until dense shade or a mechanical barrier stops it.

26. My neighbor planted zoysia, but I don't want it spreading into my lawn. What can I do to stop it?

Unless there is a driveway, walk, wall, or some other type of physical barrier between your lawns, the zoysia will eventually spread into your lawn. A metal barrier pushed into the soil will stop zoysia if you don't push the metal all the way into the ground. If you do, the stolons will grow over the top of the barrier and into your lawn. I do not know of any chemicals that will selectively kill zoysia and not harm any of the other grass in your lawn.

27. Is dichondra a grass?

Dichondra is not a grass but a ground cover. It is a close relative to morning-glory and is most commonly used in the southern portions of California. It makes a nice, attractive lawn if fertilized, mowed, and irrigated like a regular grass lawn.

But a word of warning. If you have dichondra for your lawn, remember it is a broadleaf plant and therefore any chemicals, especially 2,4-D, dicamba (Banvel D), and 2,4,5-T, that kill broadleaf weeds will also kill dichondra.

28. What is buffalograss?

This is a highly drought-resistant grass used in the hotter, arid areas of the United States where there is very little rainfall, and where irrigation is limited or not available. It thrives under close mowing and drought conditions. Too much watering, fertilization, or too high a mowing encourages weeds and other grasses to become established and cause shade problems. Buffalograss is not tolerant of shade and will quickly be crowded out by other vegetation if shady conditions persist.

29. How can I establish buffalograss in my new lawn?

Seeding or plugging can be used, depending on your own personal needs. Because of the difficulty of getting good seed, plugging or sodding would probably be the best method to use. Spot sodding (plugging) should be done in the spring, using 3-inch to 4-inch sod cubes cut thick and placed at 12-inch to 18-inch centers on a firm, level soilbed. It takes 25 to 50 square feet of sod, cut into cubes, to cover 1,000 square feet. Water should be added only in small amounts to reduce weed competition.

30. Why is redtop no longer included in grass-seed mixtures?

This grass is a poor relative to bentgrass and is now considered to be an undesirable lawn grass. It tends to grow in clumps, and its coarse leaves do not blend well with other grasses. It is some-times included with other seed because of its ability to germinate quickly and give a new lawn the appearance of having some grass present. It usually will be crowded out by the other grasses in a year or two.

31. Bentgrass makes such a nice putting green that I wonder how would it do for a regular lawn?

If you want to spend as much time and money on your lawn as a professional turf manager spends maintaining a green, bentgrass will make an excellent lawn. But remember it requires special care to keep it healthy and looking nice. Frequent mowing with a reel mower, extra fertilizer, disease and insect control, and thatch removal are just a few of the things that will keep you busy.

32. Which of the newer bluegrasses have the best chance of sur-viving in the shady areas on my lawn?

The three varieties that seem to offer the best shade tolerance are Warren's A-34, Glade, and Sodco. In tests, all have done excep-tionally well when the height of cut has been one and a half to two inches and ample fertilizer has been applied. Remember, no grass can survive in shade without your help. Proper fertilization, good watering practices, and mowing at the correct height are all important in maintaining grass in shady areas.

33. I've heard so much about Merion Bluegrass over the years. Is it still one of the best bluegrasses to buy?

Merion is the most famous relative in the bluegrass family. It was the first truly improved bluegrass to be presented for the homeowner's use back in the late forties and early fifties. Today it still ranks as one of the elite bluegrasses for home lawns, as well as on golf courses. When using any bluegrass, it is wise to seed two or more varieties, as a blend, for added insurance against disease and insect problems.

34. What is a blend of bluegrasses?

This refers to the mixing together of seed from two or more different varieties of bluegrasses. An example would be a blend containing 50 percent Merion and 50 percent Fylking.

35. How well will Kentucky bluegrass and red fescue do when seeded together?

These two grasses are quite compatible and do well together in lawns, especially in light-to-moderate shaded areas. The blue-grasses will eventually crowd out the red fescue in the open areas that receive full sunshine most of the day. But in heavy-shaded areas, the red fescue will predominate.

36. What is the advantage of using a blend when seeding my lawn?

A blend offers a homeowner some insurance against disease problems. Since each variety of grass has a different susceptibility to diseases, chances are good that any one disease will not affect all of the grass varieties in your lawn. This allows disease-resistant plants to continue normal growth and will help you maintain a more attractive lawn.

37. What is a dwarf bluegrass?

Dwarf bluegrasses are often called low growers because the grass blades tend to grow close to the surface rather than growing straight up as do the older varieties of bluegrasses. Some of the low-growing varieties available are Pennstar, Fylking, and Sodco.

38. Why would a dwarf bluegrass be used for a home lawn?

The advantages of these grasses is their ability to withstand short-mowing heights. This means a homeowner can have a manicured lawn with a short (¾-inch) cut without retarding the growth of the grass.

39. Is there a difference between tall fescue and red fescue?

Yes, there is a remarkable difference. Tall fescue has coarse, wide leaves that are not too attractive for home lawns. If you have an area away from your house that gets a lot of play, or if you live in a region where droughty conditions are a problem, you may want to consider growing tall fescue. Red fescue has a narrow, fine leaf and is often seeded alone or in seed mixtures where shade is a problem.

40. How do Bermudagrass and bluegrass growth requirements differ?

They are as dissimilar as night and day in their requirements for developing a thick, healthy lawn. The growing seasons for Bermudagrass and bluegrass are opposites.

Bermudagrass grows best in hot, summer weather, where, if adequate moisture and ample fertilizer have been applied, the lawn will have to be mowed twice a week. Mowing height for Bermudagrass is ½ to ¾ of an inch.

Bluegrasses will hardly need mowing during hot weather unless watered regularly to prevent them from becoming dormant. Bluegrass grows best in the cool spring and fall, and should be mowed regularly at 1½ to 2 inches.

41. Why is it we are able to grow bluegrass in our lawns when we live in the Southern grass region around Atlanta?

Local climatic conditions will influence the choice of grass you use in your lawn. In your case, the higher elevation and cooler summer temperatures around Atlanta allow the bluegrasses to survive.

42. Is it possible to use blends of Southern grasses in my yard?

The practice of using blends works well for bluegrasses in the Northern regions of the United States, but in the South a pure stand of one kind of grass is usually grown. The reason for this is that most of the Southern grasses are creeping varieties forming a dense, thick mat, crowding out the weakest grass in the mixture. The wide ranges in maintenance requirements of the different grasses would make it difficult for the homeowner to set up a maintenance schedule that did not favor one grass over another in a mixture.

43. Why is Bermudagrass called a creeping grass?

Creeping is a term used by many people in discussing how grasses spread into bare areas and flowerbeds by underground stems (rhizomes) or aboveground stolons. These two plant parts are capable of growing great distances away from the parent plant and sending up new grass plants all along their surface. This characteristic is a great advantage because it does give the grass the ability to spread into bare or damaged areas and thus keep the lawn looking nice. Bermudagrass, bluegrass, zoysia, bentgrass, centipedegrass, St. Augustinegrass, Bahiagrass, and a few other grasses should all be classified as "creepers."

44. Why do some of the homeowners in the South avoid having a Bermudagrass lawn?

The main drawback in using Bermudagrass for your lawn is the tremendous amount of work and money required to have it nice-looking. Most homeowners trying to grow it never realize how much care and management are really involved. Bermudagrass requires more than the usual amount of fertilizer, will not tolerate heavy shade, and needs warm weather and frequent close mowing to look its best.

45. Will Bermudagrass grow in the heavy shade under the trees on my lawn?

It will grow in the shade but will not form a dense, healthy lawn under these conditions. You would be better off to plant St.

Augustinegrass in the shade rather than Bermudagrass. Another problem with trying to grow Bermudagrass under these conditions is the soil wetness usually associated with a shaded area. A well-drained soil is a must in order to have a Bermudagrass lawn.

46. I'm getting ready to put in a new Bermudagrass lawn. Should I use common Bermuda or one of the newer varieties being advertised?

If you are going to spend very little time or money on your lawn after the grass has become established, you should use the common Bermuda variety. It requires little maintenance and will form a shaggy, but acceptable lawn.

On the other hand, if you want a lawn that reflects your pride in your home, then use one of the newer varieties available. They require much more work on your part, but the end results are well worth it. These grasses require frequent, close mowing, with ample amounts of nitrogen being needed throughout the growing season. Thatch removal should also be an important part of your annual maintenance program. Some examples of the newer, improved varieties of Bermudagrass are Tifgreen, Tifway, Tifdwarf, and Sunturf.

47. What is the best way to establish Bermudagrass in my lawn?

Too much variation occurs when seed is used to start a Bermudagrass lawn. The newer varieties on the market today have to be established from plugs or sprigs for a uniform-looking lawn.

TABLE 2–2

Vegetative Planting of Grasses

Grass	Method	Amount/1,000 Sq. Ft.
Bermudagrass	sprigs	1 bushel
Buffalograss	plugs	25 to 50 sq. ft. of sod
Carpetgrass	plugs	20 to 40 sq. ft. of sod
Centipedegrass	plugs	20 to 40 sq. ft. of sod
Zoysia	plugs	25 to 30 sq. ft. of sod

48. Should Bahiagrass be used for a home lawn where a well-manicured appearance is desired by the homeowner?

No. This grass is a moderately low-growing perennial that will do well in soils that are almost entirely sand and low in fertility.

The grass forms a coarse turf that looks good from a distance but up close does not have a dense, uniform appearance needed for home lawns. Bahiagrass may be used for a home lawn if the owner realizes that the quality of the lawn will never be topnotch.

49. What type of maintenance is necessary for a lawn that is almost entirely Bahiagrass?

One of the advantages of this grass is its ability to get by on very little assistance from anyone. It needs only small amounts of fertilizer, and it is fairly drought resistant. It does well on poor soil as well as on a good soil. The only maintenance it requires at regularly scheduled intervals is mowing. It should be clipped often at 2½ to 3 inches with a sharp mower; the clippings should be removed after each mowing.

50. Which variety of Bahiagrass is best suited for home lawns?

There are several different varieties of this grass, most of which are best suited for pasture use or along roadsides. Pensacola, Paraquay 22, Paraquay, Argentine, and common Bahia are the more common varieties on the market, with Argentine and Paraquay 22 the two used mostly for home lawns.

51. What are some of the characteristics that make St. Augustinegrass popular for Southern lawns?

Some of the reasons most often given are its ability to tolerate shade (if not too heavy), tolerance of salty soils, ability to grow well regardless of soil conditions, and its natural dark-green color, which really stands out when properly fertilized and managed.

52. How is St. Augustinegrass established into a new lawn?

Seed is not commercially available for this grass so it has to be established by vegetative propagation methods. This means sodding the entire lawn, or plugging, sprigging, or spot-sodding.

Sodding the entire lawn is expensive and therefore is usually not done. Plugging is accomplished by using 3-inch to 6-inch squares of sod and planting them in the soil on 12-inch centers. The fastest way is to use sprigs (individual stolons) and plant them end to end in rows 4 inches to 6 inches apart.

53. How much maintenance does St. Augustinegrass need?

This grass requires about as much attention as does Bermudagrass. Considerable attention must be given in order to develop it into a nice lawn. A good fertilization program, proper watering, and regularly scheduled mowing are critical if your lawn is to be thick and cushiony.

Maintenance Requirements of St. Augustinegrass

FERTILIZATION Too much fertilizer causes this grass to build up excessive amounts of thatch in short periods of time, whereas too little fertilizer will cause the grass to turn yellowish. Local climatic conditions govern the amount of fertilizer that needs to be applied. Check with a local garden center for recommendations on the proper rates for your area. A well-fed lawn will be able to withstand more abuse than a poorly fed one.

WATERING This grass requires large amounts of water to keep it growing, especially during the warmer parts of the year. When watering, apply enough to soak deeply into the soil to encourage the grass roots to grow down into the ground.

MOWING The varieties used for home lawns should be cut at a height of 1¼ to 1½ inches. If cut any shorter than this, the grass will be severely weakened and will eventually die. Using a mower with sharp blades is essential if the lawn is to look uniform. Dull blades will tear at the grass blades and give the lawn a whitish color. Since this grass builds up thatch readily, you should catch the clippings so they cannot add to this problem. Set your mower ½-inch higher than normal when mowing in shady locations: this will give the grass that extra chance to do well.

54. What pests cause the most problems on St. Augustinegrass?

Both insects and diseases can be problems if not kept under control. Chinch bugs, armyworms, and sod webworms all can do extensive damage, with the chinch bug usually being the most serious. Gray leafspot and brown patch account for a majority of the disease problems. Both diseases can be controlled easily if the chemicals are applied before the disease has done most of the damage. Weeds should not be a problem if the lawn is healthy and has been maintained properly. If used as a spot treatment, 2,4-D can be used to control broadleaf weeds. But St. Augustinegrass is susceptible to 2,4-D in large doses.

55. What are some of the characteristics of centipedegrass that make it a good lawn grass?

One feature that makes this an excellent grass is its ability to do well without much care from the homeowner. This grass spreads by stolons and has the ability to do well in any kind of soil. Although it can get by on very little fertilizer, it will perform much better if it is fed 2 to 4 times a year. Be careful not to overfertilize. It should be mowed at 1 inch to 1½ inches high but can be mowed as low as ½ inch for a highly manicured lawn. Mow high rather than short in the shade. Don't plant this grass where it will get heavy traffic, or it will wear out quickly, and recovery is usually very slow.

56. Are there any improved varieties of centipedegrass available?

Common centipedegrass is most often used, but one new variety, Oklawn, is now available on a limited basis. This new variety is more tolerant of drought and heat than common centipedegrass. It also does equally well in shade or sunlight and shows excellent resistance to insects and disease problems. Both varieties will do well as lawn grasses in the southern two thirds of the Southern grass region. The cooler temperatures found in the upper third of the region will not allow these grasses to do very well.

57. Does carpetgrass require a lot of work to keep it looking nice in a lawn?

This depends on what you consider to be "a lot of work." Generally, this grass requires very little maintenance for it to survive, but the more you do for it the better it will perform. If you follow a good fertilization program, keep it watered, and mow frequently, carpetgrass will form a dense, thick lawn. Don't try to grow this grass in shaded areas.

3

Facts on Fertilizers

58. What is a fertilizer?

Any material that contains some nutrients needed for plant growth. It can be natural material, such as manure, or it can be a manufactured material, such as ammonium nitrate. See Table 3–1 for a listing of natural and manufactured materials.

TABLE 3–1

Natural Materials	Manufactured Materials
Bone meal	Ammonium nitrate
Cocoa shells	Ammonium sulfate
Grass clippings	Superphosphate
Farm manure	Ureaform
Cotton hulls	Potash
Guano	Urea

59. What is the difference between inorganic, natural organic, and synthetic organic fertilizers?

Inorganic fertilizers are materials such as ammonium nitrate and potassium sulfate that are in a soluble salt form and that readily dissolve in water for plant use. Natural organic fertilizers are materials such as manure or guano that have to undergo decomposition to release the nutrients in a form that the plants can use. (See Table 3–2). Synthetic organic fertilizers are manufactured products that have the nutrients bonded into a carbon-hydrogen complex. This usually results in a slower, more controlled release of the nutrients over a period of time. In most cases this type of fertilizer is best for lawn use.

TABLE 3-2

Plant Food Value of Various Manures

	%			Rate Nitrogen
	N	P	K	Is Available
Horse	3	2	2½	very slow
Cow	4	1½	3	slow
Sheep	3	1½	3	slow
Chicken	6	4	2	fast

EXAMPLE: One hundred pounds of horse manure would contain 3 pounds of nitrogen (N), 2 pounds of phosphorus (P), and 2½ pounds of potassium (K).

60. How much nitrogen is there in the natural organic fertilizers?
The nitrogen content will vary, but it is usually very low (1.0 percent–6.0 percent). A large volume of material is therefore needed to supply the grass with sufficient nitrogen.

61. What do the numbers 12-4-8 represent on a fertilizer bag?
These numbers refer to the percentage of nitrogen, phosphorus, and potassium in the bag. A 50 pound bag of 12–4–8 fertilizer would contain 6 pounds of nitrogen, 2 pounds of phosphorus, and 4 pounds of potassium. The other 38 pounds are carrier material. (See fig. 3–1.)

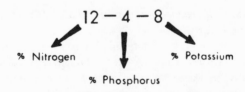

Figure 3–1. Relative percentages of the three major nutrients in fertilizer.

62. How can I tell if the fertilizer I am buying is actually for lawn use?

Usually if the fertilizer bag has the words "turf or lawn fertilizer" on it or gives the rates that the fertilizer should be put on a lawn in terms of pounds per 1,000 square feet, then chances are good it was made for use on lawns. Another check is to look at the grade (12–4–8, 18–5–9, 16–4–8) on the fertilizer bag. If the nitrogen is approximately twice as high as the potassium then it is probably a turf fertilizer. Farm-brand fertilizers that have all three numbers of the grade the same (12–12–12), or whose nitrogen source is all water-soluble, are not the best for use on home lawns. However, if this is all that is available to you, it is better than no fertilizer at all.

63. What do people mean when they speak of a fertilizer ratio and grade?

The term *grade* refers to the percentage of nitrogen, phosphorus, and potassium present in the bag of fertilizer. The term *ratio* means the proportion of these three major nutrients to one another in a bag of fertilizer. In general, the best fertilizers for lawn use have a ratio where the nitrogen is 2 to 3 times higher than the potassium. There should be less phosphorus present in the bag than potassium. See Table 3–3.

TABLE 3-3

Fertilizer

Grades and Ratios

12–12–12	1:1:1
16–8–8	2:1:1
16–4–12	4:1:3
20–5–10	4:1:2
24–4–8	6:1:2

64. What do the terms complete fertilizer and balanced fertilizer mean when found on a fertilizer bag?

Complete fertilizers are those containing nitrogen, phosphorus, and potassium, but the amounts can vary considerably. Some examples of the different grades of complete fertilizer you can buy are 16–8–8, 12–12–12, 16–4–8, 30–3–10, 18–5–9, and 16–6–4. A balanced fertilizer is one having the three major nutrients—nitrogen, phosphorus, and potassium—mixed in a ratio most beneficial for the grass. Balanced turf fertilizers would have grades similar to the following examples: 12–4–8, 18–5–9, and 30–3–10.

65. What are the important plant nutrients a lawn fertilizer should contain?

Nitrogen, phosphorus, and potassium are the three major nutrients to look for. If other nutrients are listed, consider them a bonus.

66. Why do the grass plants need nitrogen, phosphorus, and potassium?

Nitrogen causes the grass to have a deep-green color. It also stimulates good growth of the leaf and blades, producing a luxuriour lawn. Phosphorus is primarily used in developing a good root system. Potassium enables the plant to take up nutrients and gives the plant resistance to diseases.

67. Is it always necessary to use a turf fertilizer containing nitrogen, phosphorus, and potassium?

Most lawns are underfertilized. Using a complete fertilizer would certainly be beneficial. If you are sure there is an adequate supply of phosphorus and potassium in your soil, you could use a fertilizer containing only nitrogen. It would be a good idea, however, to apply a complete fertilizer to your lawn at least once a year.

68. Does the term minor element on a fertilizer bag mean the nutrients are not as important for plant growth as are the major nutrients (nitrogen, phosphorus, and potassium)?

The minor elements (nutrients) are as important for plant growth as are the major nutrients. The terms *minor* and *major* refer to the amount needed by the plants to complete a life cycle. Table 3–4 shows a list of major and minor nutrients.

69. Fertilizer is an added expense. Is it necessary?

Because fertilizing is one of the keys to having a nice lawn, it should be done. It will cause the grass to be a deep-green color, help it withstand heavy use, and keep the weeds out. With fertilization, a lawn will have a better chance of maintaining itself against all the other competition (weeds, disease, and insects).

70. What month of the year should a fertilizer be applied?

This will be determined by the weather, type of grass, and amount of water available. Grass should be fertilized at the beginning and end of the growing season. An application in the

TABLE 3-4

Major Nutrients	Minor Nutrients
Carbon	Boron
Calcium	Chlorine
Hydrogen	Copper
Magnesium	Iron
Nitrogen	Manganese
Oxygen	Molybdenum
Phosphorus	Zinc
Potassium	
Sulfur	

middle of the season is good if the weather is not too hot and there is water for irrigation. (See chapter 11 for additional information).

71. How does fertilizing in the early spring benefit my lawn?

The most important thing it does is to insure the availability of an adequate supply of nitrogen to the grass plant. This will help get your grass off to a quick start and allow it to green-up quickly in the spring. This will not only result in an attractive lawn but will also give the lawn a good head start on any weeds that are trying to get established.

72. How much fertilizer should be applied to a lawn in a single year?

This depends on the grade of fertilizer being used. Generally the rates are given as pounds of actual nitrogen to be applied per 1,000 square feet per year. Bermudagrass likes 8 to 12 pounds actual nitrogen per 1,000 square feet per year, whereas bluegrasses prefer 4 to 8 pounds actual nitrogen per 1,000 square feet per year. The fertilizer applications should be divided over the entire year. See Table 3-5 for nitrogen requirements for lawn grasses.

73. How should a fertilizer be applied?

It is essential to have uniform coverage, not only to insure good plant growth but also to avoid those embarrassing signs of mis-application of a fertilizer. The worst possible way is to fill a bucket with fertilizer and walk around the lawn tossing out handfuls at random. Incorrect fertilizing will show up quickly. Whenever you see dark-green strips in a lawn, with light-yellow strips between, you can be certain that uniform coverage of the lawn was not

TABLE 3-5

Seasonal Nitrogen Requirements for Lawn Grasses*

Grasses	Pounds of nitrogen per 1,000 sq. ft.
Bahiagrass	4–5
Bentgrass	6–8
Bermudagrass	8–12
Carpetgrass	3–4
Centipedegrass	3–4
Chewing Fescue	4–6
Kentucky Bluegrass	4–8
Red Fescue	4–6
Ryegrass	4–6
St. Augustine	4–6
Tall Fescue	3–4
Zoysia	5–6

* The exact rate of application will be determined by the climatic conditions of your area.

taken into consideration. Using a cyclone spreader is the best way to insure proper coverage of a lawn. If the drop-type spreader is used, more care must be used to avoid misapplication.

74. How can a fertilizer burn grass?

The term *fertilizer burn* refers to the situation where a granule of fertilizer (soluble salts) rests directly against the plant. The high salt concentration draws moisture from the plant cells in contact with the granule, and the cells die because of their dehydrated condition.

How to Avoid Fertilizer Burn to the Grass Plant

1. Never apply more than two pounds of nitrogen per 1,000 square feet at any one time.

2. Be sure to spread fertilizer material evenly over the lawn.

3. Do not overlap the fertilizer material when applying it or spill fertilizer on the grass.

4. Apply the fertilizer when the grass is dry.

5. Water as soon as possible after fertilizing. Try to time your fertilizer application just before a gentle rain.

75. *Is it necessary to water after fertilizing the lawn?*

Watering the fertilizer into the soil is a good way to insure there is no damage done to the grass because of fertilizer burn. If possible, fertilize ahead of a rainstorm and let nature do your work.

76. *Will fertilizing my lawn do any harm to the nearby trees and shrubs?*

Usually it won't harm them unless you get fertilizer on the leaves when they are wet. A well-fertilized lawn will usually supply enough nutrients to keep the trees and shrubs growing actively. You also need to be careful to keep the fertilizer away from your trees and shrubs if it contains a broadleaf weed killer. Remember, trees and shrubs are also broadleaf plants and are easily killed by the broadleaf herbicides.

77. *If organic material (peat, sawdust, etc.) is added to my lawn, is it necessary to fertilize?*

Yes, because the nitrogen in the soil will no longer be readily available for plant use. The bacteria in the soil will tie up the nitrogen for use in decomposing the excess organic matter. In this case it is often necessary to add extra nitrogen to a lawn so that the grass *and* the bacteria will have nitrogen available for their use.

78. *I have put several applications of nitrogen fertilizer on my lawn, but it is still yellow. What is wrong?*

If the grass has had ample nitrogen applied to it and remains a yellowish color, then chances are the nutrient you need to add is iron. Buy some iron sulfate from a local store and sprinkle some on a small area in your lawn. If the grass greens-up in 5 to 10 days, then you know iron was the missing nutrient.

79. *What do the letters UF mean in a fertilizer advertisement?*

This is an abbreviation for ureaformaldehyde, which is a synthetic organic nitrogen commonly used in lawn fertilizers.

80. *After a lawn is fertilized, how much time must elapse before children and pets are allowed on the lawn?*

If you are worried about the fertilizer doing any harm to the children and their pets, you shouldn't be. Unless there is an insecticide mixed in with the fertilizer, there is very little chance of their being harmed. So far as the children or pets doing any damage to a recently fertilized lawn, there is little to worry about so long as the grass was dry when the fertilizer was applied.

81. *Does the type of soil in my yard have anything to do with how often the lawn needs to be fertilized?*

Yes. The soil, along with the organic matter, is the agent that absorbs the fertilizer and holds it for the plant to use. If the soil has a high clay content, it will be able to hold the fertilizer longer than a soil high in sand. Therefore, you would need to apply more fertilizer to a sandy soil.

82. What problems will I have if I use farm-brand (12-12-12 and 16-8-8) fertilizer?

The biggest problem you'll need to worry about is the possibility of "burning" your lawn immediately after applying it. The form of nitrogen in these fertilizers is highly water-soluble and quick to dissolve and can easily concentrate large amounts of salts on the grass blades. This causes the burn.

Another thing to remember is that these fertilizers are very water-soluble and do not last as long. You'll therefore need to fertilize more frequently, using smaller amounts, if you want to maintain your lawn in the best shape possible.

83. My lawn is sort of off-green (yellowish) in color. What type of fertilizer can I use to green it up quickly?

You will want to use a fertilizer in which the nitrogen is highly water-soluble. This would mean that the nitrogen is in the ammonium, nitrate, or urea form. All three of these forms will quickly release nitrogen, which will be available almost immediately after the soil is watered, thus greening-up your yellowish lawn in 5 to 7 days.

84. At what rate should these quick-release nitrogen fertilizers be applied?

Never put on more than $1\frac{1}{2}$ pounds of actual nitrogen per 1,000 square feet when using these fertilizers. Avoid overlapping fertilizer patterns when applying them. Be sure to water immediately to reduce the chance of a chemical burn to your lawn. See Table 3–6.

85. Is there anything wrong with using a liquid fertilizer on my lawn?

If you think it is more convenient to apply fertilizer this way, then go ahead. You might find it is more expensive to use liquid fertilizer rather than the dry, granular forms.

86. When starting a new lawn, should I use a special type of fertilizer?

To give the seedling grass plant a better chance, a "starter" fertilizer would be helpful. This is a fertilizer low in nitrogen and

TABLE 3-6

Guide for Determining the Amount of
Fertilizer to Put on Your Lawn*

Percent of nitrogen in the bag	Amount of fertilizer to be applied per 1,000 sq. ft. to equal 1 pound of nitrogen
10	10.0 lbs.
12	8.3 lbs.
15	6.7 lbs.
18	5.5 lbs.
20	5.0 lbs.
24	4.3 lbs.
30	3.3 lbs.

* To apply 1 pound of nitrogen per 1,000 square feet using a fertilizer containing 12 percent nitrogen, you would have to apply 8.3 pounds of fertilizer. To apply 2 pounds of nitrogen, multiply 2×8.3; this shows that 16.6 pounds of the fertilizer are needed per 1,000 sq. ft. to equal 2 pounds of nitrogen per 1,000 sq. ft.

high in phosphorus and potassium. In early stages of growth the grass plant does not require as much nitrogen as it does when it is older. Instead, the younger plant requires ample phosphorus to develop good, strong roots, and potassium for strong, vigorous plants.

87. I have often seen "bargain" fertilizers for sale. Should I consider buying them since it would save me money?

Remember, there is no such thing as a "bargain" lawn fertilizer. In a fertilizer you get just exactly what you are willing to pay for. The so-called bargain fertilizers either do not contain enough plant food, or they are one of the farm-type fertilizers. You might be able to save money by using them, but be sure the fertilizer can measure up to the results you are expecting. At the end of the growing season, most garden centers discount their surplus lawn fertilizer, and this would be a good opportunity to save money by buying your fertilizer for the next season.

88. I have applied fertilizer to my lawn, and it just doesn't seem to do anything. My neighbor told me to add lime, and my lawn will look great. Is this right?

Your neighbor may or may not be right. The best way to find

out if you should add lime is to have a soil sample tested to find out if the pH is acidic (sour). If it is, then lime should be added, but to add lime without knowing the soil pH might be just a waste of your hard-earned money. The letters *pH* refer to the degree of acidity or alkalinity in the soil.

89. *I have a soil that is very acid (pH = 5.5, according to a soil test). Will this have any effect on how much fertilizer I should put on my lawn?*

The pH of the soil determines the availability of the nutrients. Therefore any time the soil has a sour (acid) condition such as yours, the nutrients needed by the grass will be affected. The ideal soil pH is 6.0 to 7.6 for grasses; in this pH range the plants are able to utilize the nutrients from the soil. At a lower pH, phosphorus, potassium, and nitrogen aren't as available to the plant, and if you don't plan on liming, then you'll have to apply a little extra fertilizer to overcome the effects of the acid soil.

90. *My soil is slightly alkaline (pH = 7.9). How can I reduce the pH to about 7.0?*

It is more difficult to lower the pH of a soil than to raise it. Any of the fertilizers having nitrogen in the form of ammonium, or other forms that break down to ammonium, can be used to lower the pH of your lawn. This way you not only supply the grass with the plant food it needs, but you also use the plant food in a form that will reduce the alkaline condition of your soil. Large amounts of elemental sulphur can be put on your lawn if you are in a hurry to change the pH of your soil. The following list of nutrients, when applied to your lawn, will help increase the acidity of the soil: ammonium sulfate, urea, ammonium phosphates, and urea-forms.

91. *How can you determine how large an area a bag of fertilizer will cover?*

To answer this question, let's assume you have bought a 40-pound bag of fertilizer with the following analysis (grade), 30–3–10, and that you want to apply 2 pounds of nitrogen per 1,000 square feet. First, determine how much nitrogen there is in the bag by multiplying the percent of nitrogen by the weight of the bag (30 percent × 40 lbs. = 12 pounds of actual nitrogen in the bag of fertilizer). Since there are 12 pounds of nitrogen in the bag, and you want to apply 2 pounds of nitrogen per 1,000 square feet, then this bag of fertilizer will cover 6,000 square feet

$$\frac{12 \text{ pounds nitrogen in the bag}}{2 \text{ pounds nitrogen per 1,000 sq. ft.}} \times \begin{array}{l} 1,000 \text{ square feet} = \\ \text{coverage of 6,000 sq. ft.} \end{array}$$

This same bag of fertilizer could be used to cover 12,000 square feet, but then you would be putting only one pound of nitrogen per 1,000 square feet. This means you would need to fertilize often (once a month) to have a nice lawn.

Summary

Step 1	percent of nitrogen in the bag	×	weight of the bag	=	actual nitrogen present in the bag of fertilizer

Step 2 $\dfrac{\text{amount of nitrogen in the bag of fertilizer}}{\text{amount of nitrogen you want to put on 1,000 square feet}} \times 1,000 \text{ sq. ft.} = \begin{array}{l}\text{area the bag}\\ \text{of fertilizer}\\ \text{will cover}\end{array}$

92. *I applied an organic fertilizer to my lawn during the cool, fall weather but did not see any green-up until warm weather the following spring. Why?*

In order for the grass to green-up, it had to be able to get the nitrogen from the soil. You applied the fertilizer too late, and the cool soil temperatures had reduced the activity of the soil microorganisms. Without these microorganisms (bacteria) to breakdown the fertilizer, the nitrogen wasn't available to the plant. In the spring, when the soil warmed up, the bacteria broke down the fertilizer, and the nitrogen was then available. When you apply organic fertilizers, the soil temperature has to be at least 50 degrees F. or warmer before the bacteria are active enough to release the nitrogen.

93. *I have heard that rain will pick up nitrogen and sulphur from the atmosphere, and this can act as a source of nutrients for plants. Is this true?*

Rainfall does accumulate small amounts of nitrogen from the atmosphere and will deposit about 5 pounds of nitrogen per year to 1 acre. The gaseous nitrogen in the atmosphere is converted to a water-soluble form whenever there is lightning, and the rain dissolves this nitrogen on its way to the earth. Sulphur and some of the other plant foods are brought back to the earth in the same manner as the nitrogen. However, they were usually released to the atmosphere in the form of smoke. In industrial areas, upward to 10 pounds of sulphur per acre can be carried to the earth by rainfall.

4

Seeding Rates and Procedures

94. When is the best time to seed a lawn?

Let nature be your guide. Seed during that part of the year when there is adequate rainfall and the temperature is best for seed germination. This will vary according to your locale. See Table 4-1 for the best seeding times.

TABLE 4-1

Best Seeding Times

Spring or early summer	*Fall or early spring*
Bahiagrass	Bentgrass
Bermudagrass	Bluegrass
Buffalograss	Chewing Fescue
Carpetgrass	Red Fescue
Centipedegrass	Tall Fescue

95. Can a general rule be given on how deep the grass seed should be put into the ground?

The depth of planting will vary depending on the size of the seed. In general, the smaller the seed, the shallower it should be planted. The smaller seed of the bentgrasses should be $\frac{1}{4}$ inch to $\frac{1}{8}$ inch deep, whereas the bigger seeds of tall fescue and ryegrasses can be as deep as $\frac{1}{2}$ to $\frac{3}{4}$ inch. Any seed exposed on the surface is most subject to drying out.

96. How can I achieve even coverage when seeding a new lawn?

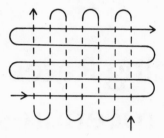

Figure 4–1. Sow seed from different directions for uni-
form coverage of lawn
area.

The best method is to cut the seeding rate in half and seed the
area first in one direction, then again at right angles to the first
direction. (See fig. 4–1.)

**97. Someone told me of a machine that does seeding. Is there such
a machine, and should I use it?**

One way of seeding, which insures the best chance of getting a
maximum amount of your seed to germinate is to rent a machine
that actually places the seed in the soil at the correct depth and
then covers it up. Since most of us do not want to rent equipment,
another way, which works very well, is to broadcast the seed over
the surface of the soil and then rake the ground lightly to help
cover the seed. A light mulch would help conserve the moisture in
the soil if you want to go to the extra time and expense. (See
Table 4–2.)

**98. How is the best way to seed small bare spots in an established
lawn?**

First, loosen the bare ground so the seed will have a good seedbed. Then hand-sprinkle the seed into the areas, followed by a
light raking to cover the seed. (See Table 4–3.)

99. Can seed be planted during the winter months?

Yes. Cold weather will not harm the dormant seed. After the
weather warms up enough to cause seed germination, moisture
becomes the most important need of the plant.

**100. What is the most common cause for new grass seedlings to
fail?**

Two things generally are at fault. Either the seedbed was not

TABLE 4-2

Standard Seeding Rates for Lawns

Type-seed	Pounds per 1,000 sq. ft.
Bahiagrass	2–5
Bentgrass	1–5
Bermudagrass	2–4
Bluegrass	2–3
Buffalograss	1–2
Carpetgrass	2–4
Centipedegrass	2–4
Chewing Fescue	3–5
Poa trivialis	2–3
Red Fescue	3–5
Ryegrass	4–6
Tall Fescue	4–6

TABLE 4-3

Seeding Rates for Small Areas
(seeds per square inch)

Kentucky Bluegrass	25 to 35
Bermudagrass	25 to 35
Bentgrass	50 to 55

prepared adequately before seeding and the seed was not placed in good enough contact with the soil, or sufficient water was not applied. The soil should be kept moist at the surface for the first few weeks until the grass is up and the roots are one inch deep into the soil.

101. What does the term certified seed refer to on a seed label?

This is the best insurance that the buyer is getting seed of the highest quality. It shows that the seed was periodically inspected, while being grown, to assure the buyer of the genetic composition and purity (weed-free) of the seed. (See Table 4–4.)

102. How can I tell when I'm getting good seed for my money?

Examine the label carefully. Look for the different kinds of grass seed present and the amount (expressed as percent of total) each contributes to the grass-seed mixture. Be sure the grasses

TABLE 4-4

Characteristics Required for Quality Turfgrass Seed

	Seed per pound	Minimum purity (%)	Minimum germination (%)
Bentgrass	8,000,000	95	90
Bermudagrass	1,750,000	95	85
Bluegrass	2,200,000	95	75
Buffalograss	45,000	85	50
Carpetgrass	1,200,000	90	90
Chewing Fescue	600,000	95	85
Dallisgrass	160,000	75	60
Red Fescue	600,000	95	85
Ryegrass	225,000	98	95
Tall Fescue	500,000	95	90

present in the mix are adapted to your individual needs. Grass seed containing crop or noxious weed seeds can introduce bothersome weeds into your lawn.

103. Is it advisable to buy lawn seed that has several different types (bluegrass, ryegrass, fescue, and bentgrass) of grass seed in it?

This would depend on where you plan to use the seed and what type of seed is present in the mixture. You would not want a seed mixture high in sun-loving grasses if you plan on using it under the heavy shade of your trees. Be sure to buy a seed mixture that meets your needs and location.

Another thing to consider when buying a mixture of seed is the width of the grass blades when the plant matures. Ryegrasses have a wide-leaf blade ($\frac{1}{8}$ inch) and red fescue a very narrow-leaf blade ($\frac{1}{16}$ inch). Mixing these two together causes a lawn to look rough (not uniform) because of the contrasting widths of the grass blades. When mixing grasses together, be sure to do so in a way that each grass complements the other and the overall effect is an attractive lawn.

104. What do the terms fine texture *and* coarse texture *refer to on a package of lawn seed?*

These terms were originally set up to separate grasses according to the width of the leaf blade when the plant reached maturity. This system of classification is no longer accurate due to the work being done in the field of plant breeding. Several of the new,

TABLE 4–5

Common and Scientific Names of Grasses*

Common Name	Scientific Name*
Annual bluegrass	*Poa annua*
Annual ryegrass	*Lolium multiflorum*
Bahiagrass	*Paspalum notatum*
Bentgrass	*Agrostis palustris*
Bermudagrass	*Cynodon dactylon*
Buffalograss	*Buchloë dactyloides*
Carpetgrass	*Axonopus affinis*
Centipedegrass	*Eremochloa ophiuroides*
Kentucky bluegrass	*Poa pratensis*
Perennial ryegrass	*Lolium perenne*
Red and Chewing red fescue	*Festuca rubra*
Redtop	*Agrostis alba*
Rough bluegrass	*Poa trivialis*
St. Augustinegrass	*Stenotaphrum secundatum*
Tall fescue	*Festuca arundinacea*
Zoysia	*Zoysia japonica*

* Notice that many of the grasses have the same first scientific name; it is therefore necessary to check the second name for positive identification.

improved ryegrasses with a narrow leaf could easily be classified as fine-textured grasses, whereas some of the newer bluegrasses could be classified as coarse-textured grasses because of their wider-leaf blade. Tall fescue, ryegrasses, and timothy are classified as coarse-textured grasses; bluegrasses, red and chewing fescues, and bentgrasses are considered fine-textured grasses. (See fig. 4–2.)

105. When buying grass seed, how much importance should I place on the amount of crop seed and weed seed present in the package?

If you want the best for your money, avoid seed mixtures that have weed seed and crop seed. Even if only small percentages (1 percent to 3 percent) are involved, you could be buying future lawn problems. For example, a 5-pound package of lawn seed, with 1 percent weed seed (*Poa annua*) and 2 percent crop seed (tall fescue), would contain 112,500 *Poa annua* seeds and 50,000 tall fescue seeds. That means a possibility of 162,500 weedy plants becoming established in your lawn. A majority of the weed and crop plants that are found in grass-seed mixtures are extremely

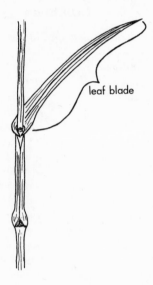

leaf blade

Figure 4–2. Location of leaf blade
on grass plant.

difficult to get out of a lawn once they become established. To avoid an unsightly lawn and a lot of hard work, pay close attention to the weed seed and crop seed present in all the lawn seed you buy.

106. When I buy 10 pounds of grass seed, how can I tell exactly how much of it will actually be good seed?

State laws require producers of grass seed to list certain items on the seed labels. Two of the items required are the percent of germination and the percent of purity of the seed. Multiply these two percentages together, and you will find out how much of your seed is good.

EXAMPLE: Suppose your 10 pounds of seed is a variety of Bermudagrass and the minimum percent of germination is 85 and the minimum percent of purity is 95. Then $85 \times 95 = 81$ percent pure live seeds, so 8.1 pounds of the seed you bought will grow under ideal conditions.

107. Should I seed or use cuttings from other plants to start my new lawn?

The easiest way to start a new lawn is to sow seed. Using cuttings (called sprigs or plugs when talking about grasses) can be very expensive and requires more time and effort on your part. When you use seed, each grass plant will have small differences in characteristics (just as each child in a family has a different personality), while a lawn established by sprigs or plugs will produce grass plants that are very similar (just like identical twins). The variations in grass plants started from seed are not too critical when using bluegrasses, fescues, and ryegrasses, but when you're seeding Bermudagrass or zoysia lawns, the variations in individual plants can be overwhelming. This is why Bermudagrass and zoysia are so often started from sprigs or plugs. Other grasses that are established by sprigging are bentgrass, centipedegrass, and St. Augustinegrass. Remember, you will be assured of getting a much more uniform lawn by using sprigs.

108. I have five pounds of grass seed left over from when I last seeded my lawn two years ago. Is this seed still good?

If the seed has been stored in a dry spot where little moisture has been present, the seed is probably still good. Seeds under these conditions remain viable for several years. To be safe, seed a little more heavily than normal to insure a good stand of grass. You should carefully measure the areas to be seeded and buy just enough to do the job. This will not only save you money but will also give you more storage room in your garage.

109. How warm does it have to be before the seed will start to germinate?

This will depend on the type of seed you are using. For bluegrasses and red fescues, the seed will start to germinate very slowly at temperatures just barely above freezing, with the optimum temperature being in the range of 55 to 60 degrees. The Southern grasses, Bermudagrass, St. Augustinegrass, and centipedegrass, will not germinate as well during the cool weather. The soil temperatures need to be about 60 to 65 degrees for best results with the Southern grasses.

110. What is the advantage of using a quick germinating grass (redtop, ryegrasses) when seeding a new lawn?

About the only advantage is the quick green-up you will get. Usually the quicker the germination, the shorter the life span. If you are seeding on a slope, the quickly established grasses will help to control soil erosion until the slower-growing grasses become established.

111. How much of the quick-germinating grass seed should there be in a good lawn-seed mixture for starting a new lawn?

The percentage should be only a small proportion of the entire mixture. Ten percent of the quick-germinating grass seed is sufficient, with any mixture containing more than 15 percent questionable for home lawns.

112. When overseeding a Bermudagrass lawn in the winter, what type of seed should I use?

When overseeding you can use bluegrass, ryegrass, or red fescue. A mixture of these three grasses will give you good results and an attractive lawn.

113. During what part of the fall should I overseed my Bermudagrass lawn?

This will be determined by when your Bermudagrass goes dormant and starts to lose its green color. In the northern part of the Southern grass region and in the higher elevations, you should be prepared to overseed by mid-October. In the warmer, southern areas, you may have to wait as late as December or the first of January before the Bermudagrass will start to lose its color. An exact date cannot be given because the grass variety and the weather affect the time when the grass becomes dormant.

114. After I prepared my lawn for seeding, it rained, and when the soil dried, there was a layer of hard, crusted soil. Can I go ahead and seed or should I break up this crust?

The crust should certainly be broken up before you seed. The crust makes it difficult for the grass seed to make good contact with the soil, and the seed that does germinate will have a difficult time getting the new roots through this hard layer of soil.

115. Should I use a mulch after seeding my lawn?

If the seedbed is adequately prepared and the seed raked into the soil and covered, it is not necessary to use a mulch. The purpose of a mulch is to shade the soil and keep the water from evaporating from the soil. This reduces the amount of time you have to spend watering your newly seeded lawn.

Straw is the most common mulch used and should be spread at about 1 to 1½ bales per 1,000 square feet. Spread at this rate, the straw normally will not have to be picked up unless it gets piled up (by the wind, people, or dogs) and begins to smother the grass. Peat moss is another mulch commonly used on new lawns. And still another good mulch is hay, which hastens germination. Whatever mulch you use, be sure that it is weed free or you will be spreading problems all over your new lawn.

116. Are there any disadvantages in mulching?

Yes. Some dry mulches, such as straw, may attract mice and insects. Straw can also be a fire hazard. Weed seeds may also be brought into your lawn by a mulch.

117. Can zoysia be put into an existing bluegrass lawn with any success?

Yes. Zoysia can be plugged (2 inches in diameter) into an existing lawn. How close the plugs are placed to each other will determine how long it takes for the zoysia to fill in. Usually 2-inch plugs, put in on one-foot centers, will fill in by the second year.

118. My Bermudagrass and zoysia lawns turn brown every winter. What can I do to keep them green if I don't want to overseed them?

If you don't want to overseed to green-up your lawn, then your only other choice is to use a turfgrass colorant and spray the grass green. There are several good turf colorants on the market; check your local garden center to find out what is available. But be prepared to take a lot of kidding from your neighbors if you use a green dye on your lawn!

119. I can think of several advantages to sodding my lawn, but what are some of the disadvantages?

The first one that comes to mind is the cost of buying sod, as compared to buying seed. The cost of sodding an entire lawn is usually prohibitive for the average homeowner. Another disadvantage, if you do the sodding yourself, is the amount of work required. But if you do sod a lawn, the transition from bare ground to a beautiful, green lawn is astounding and well worth the effort and expense.

Six Steps to Follow When Sodding Your Lawn

1. Remove all weeds, old grass, rocks, and debris.
2. Loosen up the soil to a depth of six inches.
3. Level and smooth the soil surface.
4. Apply a fertilizer on the soil surface just before sodding.
5. Lay the sod.
6. Water frequently until the new roots have penetrated into the soil.

120. When buying sod from a garden center, what should I look for to be sure the sod will send roots into the soil?

Usually a garden center will cut the sod from someplace off the premises and lay it on plastic or on the ground, where customers can readily see it. Check the edges of the sod to see if the soil has been allowed to dry out and if any of the grass has died. The grass should be a healthy green color and should have been mowed fairly short. Check the thickness of the sod. The thinner the sod was cut, the quicker the new roots will grow into the soil when the sod is laid.

121. How much watering does a newly sodded lawn require?

During the first two weeks, the sod will require large amounts of water applied daily. After the roots have gotten into the soil, then less frequent, heavy watering will force the roots deep into the soil. The slow-growing grasses, such as buffalograss and zoysia, should not be watered too heavily or weeds will become a problem. These grasses are drought tolerant and can survive on lesser amounts of water.

122. Would you recommend using a roller on newly laid sod?

A light rolling immediately after the sod has been put down will help push the sod into good contact with the soil. This reduces air pockets under the sod that could cause the sod to dry out. Rolling will also help smooth out your lawn area and eliminate the bumps. If you have the time, a light topdressing of granular topsoil will help fill in the low spots and cracks in your sodded areas.

123. How soon can new sod be fertilized?

Good quality sod has had a feeding months ahead of its cutting time. The easiest time to fertilize your new sod is right after your soil has been prepared for the sod, but before you lay the sod. This puts the fertilizer right on the soil surface, where the new roots emerging from the sod can readily get to it. The fertilizer should be put on at a rate of one pound of actual nitrogen per one thousand square feet. All the heavy watering required to keep the sod from drying out will wash much of the fertilizer away, so about two months after the sod has been down, another application of fertilizer would be beneficial.

124. On steep slopes, how can I keep the sod I'm laying from sliding to the bottom?

Always lay the sod along the slope and not in an up-and-down direction. Driving stakes into the sod and pegging it to the soil will prevent it from slipping to the bottom of the slope. Be sure the pegs are left exposed so you can pull them out after the sod has sent roots deep into the soil bank.

125. *Can I do anything to improve the clayey soil in my yard before planting a new lawn?*

Contrary to popular belief, adding sand to a clayey soil is not good. The addition of organic matter (manure, peat, compost, straw) will do more to improve the soil than anything else. The organic matter should be mixed thoroughly into the soil with a rotary tiller. When the organic matter decays, it breaks down into chemicals that bind the clay into granules, thus improving the soil. Remember, the increase of organic matter will require the lawn to be fertilized a little more often for a few years.

126. *What is a soil sterilant?*

This is a type of chemical used to kill every living thing in the soil. It is often necessary to use a soil sterilant when some undesirable weed, disease, or insect is present in your lawn. It should be noted that these chemicals are just as effective on people as they are on lawn pests and should therefore be handled with caution.

Soil sterilants can be used to solve the following problems:

1. quackgrass
2. unwanted bentgrass
3. Bermudagrass (in Northern lawns)
4. nematodes (microscopic worm-like animals)
5. soil fungi
6. soil insects
7. tree roots
8. weed seeds

127. *Will continued, heavy watering or rains hurt the new grass seedlings as they sprout?*

Yes. The water beating down on the bare soil surface tends to break down the soil, and a hard, dense crust is formed. This crust will make it difficult for the new grass to sprout. It also reduces air movement into the soil, thus slowing up the seed-germination process. This is why it is recommended to use a soft, mist spray when watering a newly seeded area for the first few weeks, at least until the grass is up.

128. *Is any special care required when mowing new grass?*

Be sure the lawn mower is sharp; a dull blade will tend to tear up the shallow-rooted grass. If the ground is extremely wet, avoid mowing rather than tracking up your new lawn and compacting the soil. Compacted soil makes it difficult for a young grass plant to survive.

129. Does soaking grass seeds before planting them shorten the time I'll have to wait to have a lawn?

Usually, presoaked grass seed will not germinate any faster than unsoaked grass seed. If you keep the soaked seed inside and at the right temperature, without letting it dry out, it will begin to germinate. This seed can then be spread on your seedbed, and it will have a small head start. However, the work involved is hardly worth the effort.

130. How can I help the Bermudagrass predominate in the spring over the grasses that were overseeded into it for a winter green-up?

First, lower your mower down to about ½ inch and mow your lawn. This will remove most of the tops of the winter grasses (bluegrass and ryegrass) and put them in a stress that weakens them. Now fertilize the lawn at twice your normal rate and water it heavily. This will cause the Bermudagrass to green-up quickly and will give it a good jump on the overseeded grasses. All this has to be done just before the Bermudagrass begins to come out of its winter dormancy.

131. Will fertilizing and seeding my new lawn on the same day hurt the grass seed?

Seeding and then fertilizing the same day will very seldom damage the grass seed. It is actually beneficial to the new lawn if the fertilizer has been applied at the time of seeding. This insures an adequate supply of nutrients being available when the new grass seedlings first start to grow.

5

Watering Your Lawn

132. When is the best time of day to water a lawn?

The best time is early in the morning when the wind is calm and the grass is already wet with dew. Usually the water pressure will be higher in the morning. Remember that keeping the grass wet for long periods of time during hot weather incubates diseases.

While morning watering is the best time slot for seeing to your lawn's needs, you should be aware that watering can be done anytime. In some cities and states, laws dictate the time of day you can water your lawn.

133. How can I tell when my lawn needs water?

The best way is to test the soil for moisture with your fingers. If the soil is dry three inches to four inches deep, then it is time to water. Another way is to keep an eye on the grass and when it shows a bluish color (wilting) or has lost its normal green color, then it is time to water.

134. How often should I water my lawn?

This is determined by the variety of grass, soil conditions, and the weather. It is best to wait until the soil has dried two inches to six inches deep; then apply enough water to soak the soil again to this depth. Watering every day is a poor practice because it favors weed growth and encourages the grass to be shallow-rooted and weak.

135. Does the type of soil in my lawn affect the watering schedule?

Yes, because the soil acts as a natural reservoir. The more clay present, the greater the water-holding capacity of a soil. A sandy soil will hold less water in the root zone. Organic matter holds large quantities of water; therefore the amount present in the soil will also influence how often you have to water a lawn. (See Table 5–1.)

TABLE 5–1

Approximate Water-Holding Capacity of Soils

Soil type	Inches of water per foot of soil depth
Sandy soils	¾ to 1
Loam soil	1 to 1½
Clay loam soils	2
Clay soils	2 to 2½

136. How much water will grass remove from the soil in a day?

This will vary depending on the type of grass, soil condition, and weather. It can generally be said that grass will remove about one-fourth inch to one-half inch of water from the soil on a hot day.

137. Is fertilizer a substitute for water?

Fertilizers should not be considered a substitute for water. The grass plant needs water regardless of the amount of fertilizer applied. Ample watering helps to dissolve the fertilizer so that its nutrients can be more easily used by the grass plant. Fertilizers are important in the greenness and rooting of the grass.

Rainfall Doubles As a Fertilizer

Rainfall is beneficial to lawns in more ways than just supplying moisture for plant growth. If you live in an area with 30 inches of rainfall per year, the rain will contribute up to 6½ pounds of nitrogen per acre. This nitrogen will be sufficient to replace any lost from the soil due to leaching.

138. Does watering during the heat of the day hurt the grass?

No. It is often very beneficial when done on extremely hot days. Watering will cool the surface temperature of the soil and will also reduce the heat stress on the grass.

139. Will the grass green-up again after it has turned brown during long, hot, dry spells in the summer?

Grass will go dormant three to five days after the first signs of its wilting. Once it has gone dormant, the addition of water will allow the grass to green-up again, but the recovery is usually very slow.

140. Is the grass harmed by letting it go dormant?

The mechanism that causes the grass to go dormant is nature's way of protecting the grass during periods of stress. The grass will recover completely, but during this recovery period, the weeds and insects have an excellent opportunity to become established in your lawn.

141. Is it true that soft water is harmful to grass?

Generally no. Soft water is merely water free of the calcium and magnesium salts. However, sodium has been added to the water in the process of removing the hard salts, and excess sodium in the soil can be harmful.

142. Why does the ground under the shade trees always dry up so quickly, even after a heavy rainstorm?

To a very large extent, the natural canopy the tree forms prevents the rainfall from penetrating the ground. This means less natural moisture accumulates under the trees, and extra water must be added by sprinklers. The roots of most shade trees are very shallow and compete with the grass for any moisture present in the soil.

143. How can I measure how much water I'm getting on my lawn when I sprinkle?

Set several cans in a straight line at different distances from the sprinkler. Run the sprinkler for one hour and then measure the depth of the water collected in each can. Divide by the number of cans used, and the answer will be how much water your sprinkler delivers in one hour. If the sprinkler delivers one-half inch of water per hour, then you would have to operate the sprinkler for two hours to get one inch of water on your lawn. The water in the cans will also indicate whether the sprinkler is distributing the water uniformly over your lawn. (See fig. 5–1).

144. I know water is necessary for a plant to live, but no one has ever told me why. Can you?

The majority of the nutrients in the soil are dissolved in water and move to the roots this way. Probably the most important function of water in a plant is the role it plays in photosynthesis. This process uses sunlight, carbon dioxide, and water and,

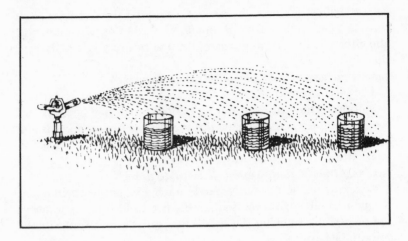

Figure 5–1. Checking water distribution from a sprinkler.

through a series of chemical reactions, produces the food the plant needs. (See Table 5–2.)

TABLE 5–2

Water Requirements of Plants

Type of Plant	Pounds of water required to produce 1 pound of dry matter
Thistles	350
Kentucky bluegrass	500
Clover	775
Lamb's-quarters	800

145. Since the top part of the plant is exposed to plenty of air, why does the soil need to have so much air in it?

The aboveground parts of a plant usually do not absorb any oxygen from the atmosphere but instead absorb carbon dioxide and in turn release oxygen back into the atmosphere. This is how your lawn is doing its share to help prevent air pollution. It not only removes pollutants (carbon dioxide) from the air but also replaces them with oxygen.

Just the opposite situation occurs below the ground level. The roots of the grass plants require oxygen to survive, and they remove oxygen from the soil air spaces. If all of the air spaces are filled with water, due to overwatering or heavy rainfall, then the roots cannot function at their best, with the upper portion of the plant suffering, turning yellow, and even dying because of the lack of oxygen.

146. How soon after I apply a pesticide may I water my lawn?

This would depend on the chemical you have applied and what pest you are trying to kill. Read the label on the pesticide container and see if it tells you when to water after applying the chemical. If you are not trying to kill a pest that lives in the soil, you probably should let the chemical dry on the plant 12 hours before watering. If you want to kill lawn grubs, cutworms, or any pest that lives in the soil, then water immediately after applying the chemical. This concentrates the chemical right in the soil where the pest will come in contact with it.

147. What are some management practices I can use to reduce the amount of water needed by my lawn?

Mowing your grass at the proper height is a good start. Mowing too short puts the grass under a stress and causes it to use more water to overcome it. Overwatering reduces root growth. Moreover, the plant is capable of absorbing more water than it actually needs, so to prevent the plant from wasting water, do not overwater. Proper fertilization will help to conserve water. Overfertilizing stimulates the grass to grow rapidly and causes it to require larger quantities of water.

148. Why does the grass always turn brown so quickly next to the south side of the house?

There is a good chance that, when the foundation of your house was built, the contractor filled along the wall with rocks, boards, and other odd bits of construction material. Often this is done to within a few inches of the surface of the ground, then covered with soil, tamped, or water-soaked to settle the area. This compacted soil does not absorb water very readily, so the grass plant has a difficult time growing in it.

Two other factors that could be involved in this problem are the eaves on your house and the sunlight. The eaves keep the rain water from dripping on the ground next to the house, especially since most houses have rain gutters on them. This means there is a natural tendency for areas next to the house to dry out more quickly than the rest of your lawn. The sun adds to the problem by reflecting off the side of your house and evaporating the water from the soil next to it.

149. What is the best type of lawn sprinkler for watering my yard?

Each of the several different types on the market today does an adequate job provided you make sure the water coverage is correct. Two of the better types are the oscillating-wave sprinkler and the impulse-oscillating sprinkler.

The wave type often soaks the soil the deepest near its base, so when it is reset to a new location you should allow for a 50 percent overlap of the last sprinkler pattern. The impulse-oscillating sprinkler does a good job of wetting the soil evenly unless there is a strong wind or a slope. Regardless of the type of sprinkler you use, put some cans out and test the coverage.

150. Does it matter what size hose I use when watering the yard?

Garden hoses usually come in two standard sizes: ½-inch diameter and ¾-inch diameter. You should select a hose that is the same size as your water pipes. If the hose is smaller, you decrease the water pressure and volume of the water moving through the hose. This means you won't get as large an area watered per sprinkler setting, and it will take longer to water your lawn.

151. I would like to install an underground sprinkler system in my lawn. Is it reasonable to think I can do it myself?

Yes. You can rent a trencher, buy the pipe and necessary fittings, and install your own underground system, but you better be sure you know what you are doing before you start. Poor sprinkler coverage, low-water pressure at the end of a line, and an insufficient water supply can cause your sprinkler system to fail if you have not sized all the pipe and sprinkler heads correctly. My advice is to let a professional irrigation company design the system for you; then the chances of a self-installed sprinkler system working correctly are good.

152. A salesman told me to be sure and use a vacuum breaker when I installed my underground sprinkling system. What is a vacuum breaker?

Vacuum breakers are specialized valves that stop irrigation water from flowing back into the potable water supply. State and federal laws require the use of vacuum breakers to prevent the contamination of city water supplies.

153. What type of pipe should I use for my underground sprinkling system?

There are three types of piping material you can choose from—galvanized pipe, copper tubing, and plastic pipe. Three good reasons why you should consider not using metal pipes: (1) it will cost you more for the material, (2) metal piping is more difficult to work with, and (3) the metal piping will eventually corrode and begin leaking.

Plastic piping is the best product on the market for underground installations of irrigation systems. It is inexpensive, easy to work with, and does not corrode. Special plastic fittings are available, so you don't have to be an expert plumber to work with this type of piping.

154. What can I do to help the water soak into my lawn instead of puddling and running off into the street?

If the water cannot penetrate into the soil fast enough to prevent runoff, try punching holes into the soil. This will allow the water to move into the soil more quickly. Another solution to the problem is to apply the water slowly as a gentle spray rather than rapidly as big droplets. You will have to leave the sprinkler longer in each spot, but you will not waste as much water and you will save money.

155. I have read that I could add soap to my water and thus help the water penetrate into the soil. Is this true?

The use of surfactants (chemicals that increase the penetration ability of water) is a common practice by professional turf people, but they use a surfactant only for highly specialized reasons. A small amount of soap in your water may act as a surfactant, but actually there seems to be very little advantage in using a surfactant on home lawns.

156. What are some of the problems caused by overwatering a lawn?

Overwatering causes the grass to be shallow-rooted, which means it will wilt easily in hot weather. Waterlogging a soil encourages water-loving plants (nut sedge, annual bluegrass, bentgrass, and nimblewill) to invade your lawn. Another major problem is an economic one. Overwatering is hard on your pocketbook and your water supply.

157. Can frequent watering of a lawn also damage it?

Yes. Frequent watering also encourages the grass to be shallow-rooted. Small amounts of water applied too frequently may result in annual weeds (crabgrass, shepherd's-purse, button weed, and verbena) and once they germinate, these weeds quickly become established in your lawn and become a nuisance.

158. Can you tell me how much water the grass growing under a tree requires?

A very general rule you can use is to water the grass growing underneath your trees twice as much as the grass out in the open areas. This will supply the trees, as well as the grass, with the water they need.

159. Are there any grasses that require very little water to survive extremely hot weather?

Bermudagrasses and bluegrasses require constant watering throughout the growing season or they go dormant and turn brown. The same is true of most of the Southern and Northern grasses. In the arid parts of the United States, there are grasses that can survive on very little water; however, most of them are not very attractive and do not make a nice lawn. Nevertheless, these grasses (crested wheat, buffalograss, lovegrass, and the gamma grasses) can be used for lawns where water is scarce.

160. Does the way I mow my lawn have any affect on how frequently I should water the grass?

Definitely! The height of cut and frequency with which you mow your lawn both affect how often you will have to water your lawn. Close (short), frequent mowing causes the root system of a grass to be very shallow, thus reducing the area it can draw moisture from. Mow your grass high and less frequently, and the grass roots will go deeper into the soil, increasing the area in which they can draw moisture, and lengthening the time between waterings.

161. Can I add fertilizer to the water so that as I sprinkle my lawn I will also be fertilizing it?

This can be done if you have the proper equipment. Greenhouses use this procedure frequently, but for a home lawn it is not very practical. It requires an understanding of how to mix the water and fertilizer in the correct proportions, and complete attention while the operation is in process.

162. Water is extremely expensive where we live (desert area), and the heat during the day is unbelievable. What, besides grass, can I use?

In the hot, arid regions this is a very common problem, and many people solve it by not growing grass. Some have rock and cactus gardens, while others have spread small (pea-size) gravel and sprayed it green to give the appearance of a lawn. If water is scarce and you don't want to grow grass, then you are limited as to what you can do.

163. *I read where you can literally drown your lawn by overwatering. How is this possible?*

It may seem ridiculous, but you definitely can drown your grass by watering too much. Oxygen is necessary if a plant is to survive, and the roots of the grass plant remove oxygen from the soil. If the water forces all the air out of the soil, the plant cannot survive and slowly dies from the lack of oxygen.

164. *What are some of the advantages to having an underground sprinkler system?*

There are several advantages, but the two most important ones are the reduction in cost and the decrease in labor in watering your lawn. Usually an underground system allows you to water your entire lawn uniformly and reduces oversoaking of some areas and underwatering of others. The time saved in dragging hoses around your lawn and having to constantly check the sprinklers gives you more time for other activities. Another advantage is that the beauty of your lawn is not marred by having sprinklers and hoses all over the yard.

165. *What does my neighbor mean when he says his new sprinklers have pop-up heads?*

Pop-up is a term used for sprinkler heads that are flush with the ground until the water is turned on. The water pressure forces the sprinkler heads to pop up out of the ground about two to three inches. When the water is turned off, the sprinkler heads fall flush with the ground and are out of the way for mowing and other yard activities.

6

Mowing Practices

166. Does it hurt anything to cut my grass in the same direction every time I mow my yard?

Mowing the grass in the same direction all the time tends to cause tracks, matting, and streaking. It is best to cut the grass from different directions. Mow back and forth across your lawn from the east and the west. The next time you mow, cut the grass in a north and south direction.

167. How often should I mow my lawn?

The more often a lawn is mowed, the better it will appear. The scheduling of mowing cannot be done on a weekly or even a daily routine. It should be determined by the growing rate of your grass. A good rule to follow is not to cut off more than one half of the leaf blade at any one mowing. (See fig. 6–1.)

168. Should a lawn be mowed at the same height all year?

If you are willing to take the time to adjust your mower, you should cut the grass a little longer in the summer and shorter in the spring and fall. If any area is used for play by children or is under heavy shade, then mow the grass longer than normal. For a formal area in a sunny spot of your lawn, you can cut the grass a little shorter for the manicured look.

169. How soon will I have to begin mowing after the new grass comes up in my lawn?

This will vary for different grasses, but you should begin mowing as soon as there is sufficient growth. Let the rule on not removing more than one half of the leaf per cutting act as a guide to the first mowing.

MOWING

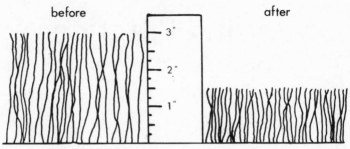

Figure 6–1. Optimum height of grass after cutting.

170. Does the type of grass have anything to do with the height of cut?

Yes. To maintain a dense turf cover, mow the grass at the height it will do best. If the grass is allowed to grow too long or if it is cut too short, you will not get the expected results. (See Table 6–1.)

TABLE 6–1

*Mowing Heights of Various Lawn Grasses**

Bermudagrass (common)	1–1½″
Bermudagrass (hybrid)	½–1″
Carpetgrass	1½–2″
Centipedegrass	1½–2″
Kentucky bluegrass (common)	2–2½″
Kentucky bluegrass (improved)	¾–1″
Red fescue	2–2½″
Ryegrass	2–2½″
St. Augustinegrass	1½–3″
Tall fescue	2½–3″
Zoysia	¾–1½″

* When the weather turns hot, it is a good idea to raise the height of cut of all grasses by at least ½ inch.

171. Is it necessary to remove the clippings from my lawn after each mowing?

If the clippings are heavy, they should be removed so that the grass is not smothered and a heavy thatch does not develop. If the grass is cut often, it is not necessary to remove the clippings; normal decay and earthworm activity will dispose of the clippings. Under these circumstances you might want to dethatch your lawn every year or two.

172. Should I leave my grass long or cut it short before the first winter snows?

Leaving the grass long is a poor practice. It can become matted over the winter and smother the grass. Long, matted grass is more susceptible to disease in the spring than is a short-cut lawn. By mowing the grass short, you allow the spring sunshine to warm up the ground quickly, thus allowing the grass to begin growing earlier in the spring.

173. What causes the tips of the grass in my lawn to turn a whitish color a few days after mowing?

This is caused by a dull mower that is tearing the blades of grass rather than cutting them smoothly. This tearing action bruises and kills the grass blades at the point of removal and causes the plant cells to die, resulting in a white, frayed appearance.

Worn or improperly sharpened mower blades cause:

1. loss of power,
2. excessive vibration,
3. improper "lift" of grass as it is cut,
4. poor discharge of cut grass, and
5. clogging of mower housing.

174. Is a reel or a rotary mower best for mowing my lawn?

This is a matter of personal opinion and what you want from a lawn mower. A reel mower is more difficult to sharpen and keep adjusted than a rotary mower. The rotary mower cuts off stemmy plants, whereas a reel mower will usually roll over them without cutting them off. The reel mower, if properly adjusted and sharpened, generally does a better job of cutting the grass and gives a more manicured look to a lawn after a mowing. The rotary mower is more dangerous to use because of its tendency to sling foreign objects, such as rocks, wire, and sticks.

Special Mower-Winterizing Instructions

Tune-up the engine.
Sharpen and balance the blade.

Check and clean the fuel system.

Check and clean the electric system.

Change the oil.

Lubricate before storing for the winter.

175. Are there any special factors to be taken into account when deciding on whether to buy a reel or a rotary mower?

Probably the most important thing for you to consider is your own mechanical ability. Reel mowers are much more complicated and require fine adjustments. If you are not mechanically inclined, these adjustments can be difficult. If you are a good mechanic and like to tinker around with equipment, then a reel mower might be just the thing for you.

176. What are some simple maintenance practices a homeowner should perform on his lawn mower?

The following maintenance practices will insure your lawn mower of a longer service life to you:

1. Check the oil frequently and add or change it as required.

2. Sharpen the mower blade(s) frequently.

3. Check the air filter for cleanliness.

4. Wash the mower off with water after each use. (Avoid getting water on the hot engine head.)

5. Store the mower inside a shelter when it is not being used.

6. Touch up the mower with paint when necessary.

177. I understand there are chemical growth retardants that will slow the growth of grass. Could I spray these chemicals on my lawn so I wouldn't have to mow so often?

It is true that these growth retardants will slow the growth rate of a grass plant, but it is not advisable for the homeowner to use them. As the grass is retarded (actually weakened), the weeds are not affected and will take advantage of the weakened grass. Often when the grass is not growing normally, there is a tendency to forget about watering, which again encourages weed establishment in a lawn.

178. When is the best time to mow a lawn?

The best time to mow a lawn is during the late afternoon or early evening when the grass is dry and the heat and humidity are not too high. The cooler part of the day is easier on the person mowing the lawn.

179. While I'm working on the undercarriage of a mower, is there

any way to insure that the engine will not kick-over and cause the blade to turn?

Every year people lose fingers by being careless when working on lawn mowers. These accidents could be avoided if simple safety precautions were taken. Always turn the lawn mower to the *off* position, even though the machine is not running, and then disconnect the spark-plug wire. Be sure the disconnected wire cannot accidentally come into contact with the spark plug. Following this procedure greatly reduces the possibility of an accident.

Fifteen Lawn-Mower Safety Tips That Could Save a Life

1. Read the owner's manual so you can understand how to operate the mower.

2. Do not allow children to play in the yard while you are mowing.

3. Never fill the gas tank in enclosed areas such as garages or sheds.

4. Children should not be allowed to operate the mower unless they are old enough to have been instructed on how to operate it. A lecture on lawn-mower safety should be included in the instructions.

5. Pick up all foreign objects (rocks, boards, twigs, toys) from the lawn before mowing.

6. Always turn the engine off when adjustments need to be made.

7. Never pull a lawn mower; always push it.

8. Do not walk away from the law mower with the engine still running.

9. Avoid storing gas and oil in unmarked containers, especially pop bottles.

10. Daydreaming is dangerous; do not do it while mowing your lawn.

11. Do not start the engine in a building.

12. Gas should never be added while the engine is running or hot. Fill the tank before starting each time.

13. Wear shoes and long pants or slacks when mowing.

14. Stay clear of the discharge chute when mowing.

15. Disconnect the spark plug when working on a lawn mower.

180. What are some suggestions for maintaining my lawn mower in tiptop condition?

1. Keep the gas free of foreign objects (grease, dirt, grass, etc.).

2. Never leave the gas tank empty after mowing because this allows condensation to occur. Once water gets into the gas system, the internal parts of the engine can become rusted, thus reducing the life of your mower.

3. Clean the air breather often. Insufficient air will cause the mower to run roughly if the breather is clogged with dirt and grass clippings.

4. Check the oil often and change it when it is dirty.

5. Clean the matted grass from the undercarriage often.

6. Check the engine mounts frequently. If the nuts have come loose, the engine vibration can literally shake your mower to pieces.

181. Is it true that shorter-than-usual mowing in the spring will cause the lawn to green-up more quickly?

During the winter months the older grass leaves will die and turn brown. In the spring the new growth will be found at the base of the old leaves. By lowering the height of cut on your mower, you can remove all the older brown leaves, thus allowing the spring growth to emerge more quickly. Be sure to catch the clippings because of the excessive amount of grass being cut at this lower height. After the lawn has been mowed once at this lower cut, return the mower to the normal height of cut.

182. How can tree damage caused by lawn mowers be reduced?

The best way is by simply being careful when mowing around trees, especially trees with a diameter of less than four inches. Usually the bark is very tender and can easily be peeled off when hit by a lawn mower. If you want to improve the beauty of your lawn and at the same time protect your trees, dig out a small circular area around your tree. Be sure to keep the weeds out by spading the soil often. If desired, the soil could be removed from around the tree and a mulch (bark or rock) put in four inches deep.

183. What can I do to reduce the amount of time required to mow my lawn?

The mowing of a lawn usually requires extra time because of a lack of planning when the lawn was put in. To reduce the amount of time it takes to mow, you can (a) put blacktop or concrete strips against all walls and under fences, (b) keep the grass surfaces even with the patio and driveway, (c) leave open areas of grass that are easy to mow, (d) install grass barriers to reduce hand trimming along flower beds, (e) use ground cover on very steep banks, (f) keep open areas of lawn free of obstacles, and (g) space trees and shrubs far enough apart so the mower will be able to get through.

184. I like to mow my grass short. Is this all right?

One advantage to mowing your grass short is that it causes the grass to tiller profusely; that is, send out new shoots from the base of the plant. However, continuous short mowing weakens the grass plants, causing shallow roots and thus inviting disease and weed problems. To overcome these problems, you need to fertilize and water more frequently and possibly spray occasionally for disease and insects. If continued short mowing is to be practiced, then a reseeding program will also need to be initiated. The low-growing bluegrasses are ideal if you live in regions 1, 2, and 3 (see the map on p. 10.)

185. What is the main reason for mowing a lawn?

The primary reason is to produce an even-looking, attractive lawn that compliments your home. Peope often judge the home-owner by the appearance of the lawn.

186. I have heard that the longer the grass is cut, the better it can withstand the heat on hot days. Is it true? And if so, why?

Yes. Longer grass will help shade the soil, thus cooling it and the microclimate (the small area where the grass plant lives). Because the soil is cooler, the grass can better survive hot weather.

187. Should I buy a self-propelled or a push-type power lawn mower?

If you have a lawn with a lot of open spaces, or if the lawn is hilly or rough, then you should consider a self-propelled lawn mower. If the lawn is large enough, you might prefer a riding mower. Both the rider mower or the self-propelled mower will reduce the amount of work involved in mowing your lawn. If your yard is small, with a lot of shrubs and trees to mow around, then the push-type power mower would be a better choice for you. This type of mower is also less expensive to buy and easier to maintain.

188. What size lawn should I have before I consider buying a riding mower?

Usually a lawn smaller than ⅓ of an acre (14,520 square feet) can easily be mowed using a push-type power mower. If your health will not allow you to walk that much, then buy a riding mower or hire someone to do the job for you. Whenever a lawn is larger than ⅓ of an acre, a riding mower should be considered, allowing the grass to be mowed in a shorter length of time. Often the riding mower has several accessories (leaf pickup attachments, snow blade, trailer) that could be of special interest to you.

189. What safety features should I look for in a lawn mower when I am buying one?

There should be a foot guard on the back of the walk mower so your foot can't slip under the mower. Controls should be within easy reach so you can turn off the engine quickly. A deflector bar at the discharge shoot is necessary to keep flying objects from being hurtled out and hurting someone. Always check the safety features before buying to insure the mower is safe to operate.

190. What, besides safety features, should I look for in a lawn mower?

1. The ease with which a mower can be started is important. An electric starter or crank starter makes this task a pleasure. 2. Consider the width of cut. The narrower it is, the longer it will take you to mow your lawn. Most push mowers are 19 to 21 inches wide. 3. The mower should have easy cutting height adjustments. 4. Check the wheel bearings; plastic ones wear out quickly. 5. Do not overlook the maintenance features of the mower. Be sure you can handle the repairs yourself; maintenance costs can be expensive if done in a lawn mower repair shop. 6. One final point: check how quietly it runs. Noise pollution today is bad enough without increasing it with a noisy lawn mower.

Facts to Contemplate About Lawn Mowers

1. Approximately 45 million dedicated homeowners mow their grass every week.

2. Some industrial experts estimate there is one mower for every five people in the United States.

3. Rotary mowers account for 80 percent of the mower sales.

4. The cutting blade of a rotary mower spins at a speed of over 195 mph when cutting grass.

5. There are approximately 125,000 lawn-mower-related accidents each year.

6. Rocks or any debris picked up and slung by mowers can reach speeds equal to the velocity of a bullet.

7. Close to 100 different companies in the United States manufacture all mowing equipment used by the homeowner.

191. I have heard you should always take a leisurely walk around the yard before mowing. What does this accomplish?

Besides giving you a little more exercise, it can reduce the possibility of an accident when you are mowing. While taking the leisurely walk, look over your lawn for foreign objects (toys, balls, rocks, wire, sticks, etc.) and remove any you find. This reduces the chances that the mower will pick up the object and hurl it through the air.

192. I have been told to wear golf shoes while mowing my yard. Is there any advantage to doing this?

There is no real advantage to wearing golf shoes while mowing a lawn. The reason people give for the suggestion is that the spikes will help improve your lawn by penetrating the grass and aerifying the soil. (See question number 328, Chapter 10.) This is not very likely to happen, since the spikes on the shoes are not long enough to penetrate the grass, let alone the soil. One exception to this would be if your lawn is so sparse that the soil can easily be seen; then the spikes could penetrate the soil. However, under these conditions, the benefit of the spiking would be overshadowed by the soil compaction caused by walking on the lawn. If your lawn is this sparse, then something else needs to be done to it other than wearing golf shoes when you are mowing.

193. Does it hurt anything to mow when the grass is wet?

Mowing when the grass is wet will not harm the grass, but it can make the job difficult and do some damage to the lawn mower. The wet grass will cause the mower to clog up much more easily than dry grass, and wet grass tends to stick to the undercarriage of your mower and make it more difficult for the engine to run at its best. If you must mow a wet lawn, do reduce the width of the swath you cut.

194. What are some of the advantages and disadvantages of an electric mower?

Some of the advantages are 1. silent running, 2. starts easily, 3. no exhaust, 4. motor seldom breaks down, and 5. no gas or oil to buy. Three main disadvantages are 1. electric cord required, 2. electrical outlets are needed conveniently located outside, and 3. trees, shrubs, and buildings cause problems with the electrical cord.

195. If the electric lawn mowers have so many advantages, why do you see more gasoline-powered mowers?

The primary reason is that gasoline models are self-contained units that can go almost any place you want. The mobility of an electric mower is greatly restricted by the length of your extension cord.

196. Does the height I mow my grass have any effect on how often I should water my lawn?

Yes. The higher the grass is allowed to grow, the more shade it will provide to protect the soil reservoir from the heat of the sun. The shade helps to keep the soil cool during the day, and this reduces the water lost from the soil reservoir by evaporation. The grass blades will also absorb some of the sun's rays as well as reflect the sun's rays away from the soil, helping to keep the soil cool. The prevention of water evaporation from the soil by mowing the grass at a high setting will decrease the amount of watering you will need to do. A grass that is mowed at a high setting will produce a root system that penetrates the soil deeper than a grass mowed at a low setting. The deeper root system has a larger soil reservoir to draw from than a shallow-rooted grass. Mowing your grass at a higher setting then allows your grass to go longer between waterings.

197. How does mowing a lawn help control leafy weeds?

Most broadleaf weeds produce new growth from the top part of the plant. In mowing you remove the growing points; this weakens the weedy plant and places it under a stress. The grass can then crowd the weakened weeds out of your lawn. Do not mow the grass too short, or low-growing weeds (chickweed, knotweed, spurge) will be able to compete with the grass.

198. Why doesn't mowing have the same affect on grasses as it does on broadleaf weeds?

The growing points (crown) of grasses are located close to the ground so the mower is always cutting off the older portion of the grass blades. Since the growing points are never removed, new growth can be produced to replace the leaf blades mowed off each week. This is similar to the way your hair grows after you have had it cut.

199. What does the term scalping mean, and how does it damage a lawn?

The term *scalping* refers to a mower set so low it cuts just above the ground level. The damage done varies from putting a stress on the plant because of the reduced leaf surface to completely killing the plant by cutting off the growing point (crown) of the grass plant. Scalping a lawn should be avoided.

200. *How is the best way to mow the bank in my front yard, up and down or sideways along the bank?*

When mowing a slope with a walk mower, always mow sideways with the slope. This reduces the chance of an accident. Riding mowers can tip over easily on a slope, so you should always mow up or down when using this type of mower on a slope.

201. *How can I check my mower to be sure it is cutting at the correct height?*

The easiest way to determine the height of cut your mower is set at is to place it on a flat surface (sidewalk) and measure the distance from this surface to the lowest point on the cutting blade. Remember to disconnect the spark-plug wire before you start.

7

Weeds and
Their Control

*202. I have heard some people call Kentucky bluegrass a weed,
yet I am enjoying my bluegrass lawn. What would be a good definition of a weed?*

The definition used most often describes a weed as any plant
growing where it is not wanted. This means Kentucky bluegrass is
a weed when growing in a flowerbed. And patches of bluegrass in
a Bermudagrass lawn would also be considered weeds.

*203. What is the difference between an annual and a perennial
weed?*

An annual weed (knotweed, purslane, sandbur, crabgrass) is a
plant that starts its growth from a seed each year. Perennial weeds
(dandelions, ground ivy, thistle, quackgrass) come back each year
from the old parts of the plant, usually from a stem or root.
Knowing which plants are annuals and perennials is important in
ridding them from your lawn. (See Table 7–1.)

TABLE 7–1

Examples of Preemergent and Postemergent Weed Killers

Preemergent	Postemergent
Dacthal (DCPA)	2,4-D
Balan (benefin)	2,4,5-TP (silvex)
Bandane	MCPP
Tupersan (siduron)	Dicamba (Banvel-D)
Betasan (bensulide)	
Azak (terbutol)	

204. Why is it important to know whether a weed is an annual or a perennial?

It is necessary to know the difference in order to properly select a weed killer to control the weeds in your lawn. Annuals die each year and reestablish themselves from seeds the following year. Many chemicals (preemergent) are formulated to stop the seed from germinating and thus eliminating the pesty weed. This type of chemical will also kill the seedlings of the perennial plants, but the original plant will still survive. It takes another type of chemical (postemergent) to control established annuals and perennials.

205. What is a preemergent weed killer?

This type of chemical kills the seeds as they germinate, preventing the plants from becoming established. To be effective it should be applied before the seed-germination process begins. Crabgrass and chickweed can be controlled by this method.

206. What is a postemergent weed killer?

Any chemical that kills growing plants is a postemergent weed killer. The most common chemical in this group is 2,4-D, and it is frequently used to control dandelions.

207. What is the difference between a broadleaf and a narrowleaf weed, and why is it important to know the difference?

The actual width of the leaf has nothing to do with the terms *broadleaf weeds* and *narrowleaf weeds*. Narrowleaf is a common term used for grassy weeds such as annual bluegrass and crabgrass. Broadleaf refers to plants such as dandelions and plantain. It is necessary to be able to identify the plants so that the proper chemicals can be used to control them. Many chemicals will control weeds of one group only, either the narrowleaf or broadleaf weeds.

208. What does the term active ingredient refer to on a can of weed killer?

Active ingredient (A.I.) is a term used to show the percentage of the solution that actually kills the weeds. If the A.I. of a gallon of weed killer is 25 percent, then one quart is the actual amount of weed killer present. The other three quarts act as a carrier. Usually the higher the percentage of active ingredient present in a mixture, the more economical it is to use.

209. How do I know which weed killers will control the weeds without damaging any of the grass, trees, shrubs, or flowers?

The safest way is to read the directions on the label and check for a listing of the plants that are susceptible to damage by the chemical. Follow the instructions carefully because some plants will tolerate only small amounts of the chemical being applied.

210. When I'm applying chemicals to control weeds, is it okay to increase the rates of application to insure the eradication of the weeds?

The best policy to follow when using any chemical is to follow the standard directions on the label. Several years of research have gone into the developing of each chemical, and the rates suggested on the label have been found to be the best. Sometimes increasing the amount of chemical applied will be harmful to the grass.

211. When is the best time to control common lawn weeds?

When you are dealing with annual weeds, the easiest time to control them is when the seeds germinate. Perennial weeds present more of a problem but can be controlled anytime they are actively growing by the application of a foliar herbicide (weed killer). Some weeds are more resistant than others to foliar sprays and may require repeated applications before they are killed. (See Table 7–2.)

212. What are some of the lawn-management practices that help control weeds?

The first rule to remember is that chemicals are not a substitute for good lawn care. Mowing, fertilization, and watering, if done properly, will help prevent weeds. Mowing the grass at the correct height allows it to become thick and prevents weeds from getting established in your lawn. This is especially true (mowing height) if there has not been any fertilizer applied or if the lawn is improperly watered. Overseeding, aerification, and dethatching also help to keep a lawn vigorous and weed free.

Three Steps to a Weed-Infested Lawn

1. Never bother to fertilize your lawn.
2. Hand-sprinkle often, just barely wetting the surface of the ground.
3. Always mow the grass as low as the mower can be set.

213. Are there any precautions I can take to keep weed seeds out of my lawn?

Here are four rules to follow for keeping weeds from getting established in your lawn:

1. When buying topsoil, be sure it has not been covered with

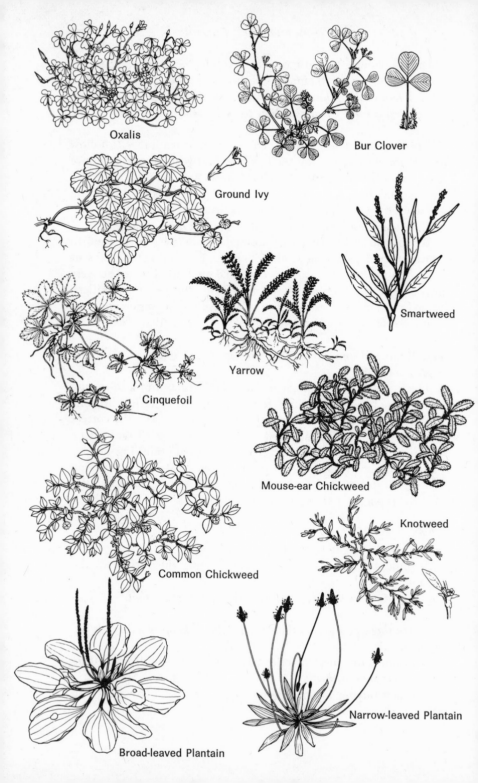

Oxalis

Bur Clover

Ground Ivy

Smartweed

Cinquefoil

Yarrow

Mouse-ear Chickweed

Common Chickweed

Knotweed

Broad-leaved Plantain

Narrow-leaved Plantain

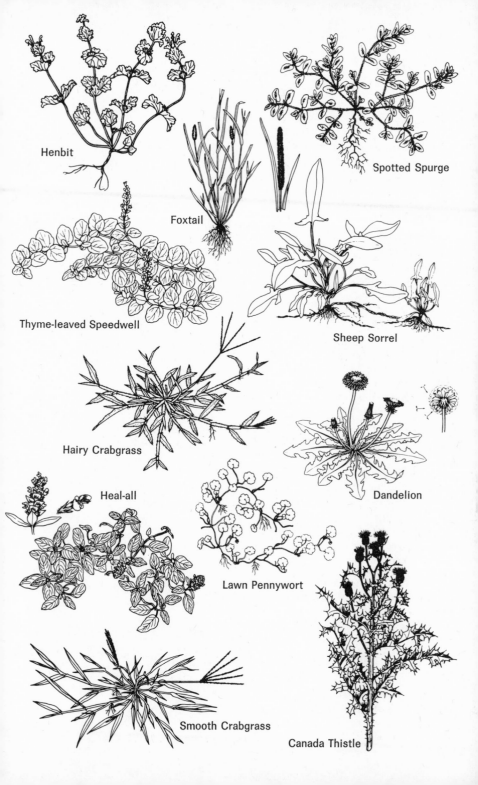

Henbit

Spotted Spurge

Foxtail

Thyme-leaved Speedwell

Sheep Sorrel

Hairy Crabgrass

Dandelion

Heal-all

Lawn Pennywort

Smooth Crabgrass

Canada Thistle

TABLE 7–2

Troublesome Lawn Weeds

	Type of Weed	Life Expectancy	When to Control	Method of Control
Barnyardgrass	N	A	S	Pre
Black Medic	B	A	S	Post
Carpetweed	B	A	S	Pre
Chickweed,				
common	B	A	S & F	Post
mouse-ear	B	P	S & F	Post
Crabgrass,				
hairy	N	A	S	Pre
smooth	N	A	S	Pre
Curly Dock	B	P	S & F	Post
Dallisgrass	N	P	F	Post
Dandelion	B	P	S & F	Post
Foxtail	N	A	S	Pre
Goosegrass	N	A	S	Pre
Ground Ivy	B	P	S	Post
Heal-all	B	P	S	Post
Henbit	B	A	S	Pre
Knotweed	B	A	S	Post
Nimblewill	N	P	S & F	Post
Plantain	B	P	S & F	Post
Poa annua	N	A	S & F	Pre
Purslane	B	A	S	Post
Quackgrass	N	P	S & F	Post
Sandbur	N	A	S	Pre
Speedwell	B	P	F	Post
Spurge	B	A	S & F	Post
Thistle	B	P	F	Post
White clover	B	P	S & F	Post
Yarrow	B	P	F	Post

N = narrowleaf, B = broadleaf, A = annual, P = perennial, S = spring,
F = fall, Pre = preemergent, Post = postemergent

weeds. Weeds growing on topsoil is an indication that weed seeds
are present.

2. Buy grass seed that is free of weed seeds.

3. When using mulches (straw and peat), be sure they are free
of weed seeds.

4. Follow good lawn-care practices to insure a luxurious lawn.

How Weed Seeds Are Introduced into Your Lawn

1. poor quality lawn seed
2. mulching material
3. topsoil used to level lawn
4. animals, especially birds
5. wind carried
6. heavy rains
7. borrowed lawn equipment
8. people (seeds stuck to clothing)

214. How can I control broadleaf weeds around trees, shrubs, and flowers when the same chemical that kills the weeds is also harmful to the desirable plants?

Often it is necessary to hand-pull many of the weeds when they are too close to desirable plants. If you want to spray the weeds, pick a day when there is no wind. Use a large piece of cardboard to shield the desirable plants as you spray the weeds. Be sure to read the instructions before starting so you understand what the chemical will and will not kill.

You could also use a wax bar, which has the herbicide impregnated into the wax. This bar can be pulled across the lawn, killing only the weeds it comes in contact with. (See Tables 7–3 and 7–4 for broadleaf weeds common to your region.)

TABLE 7–3

Broadleaf Weeds Common to the Northern States

Black Medic	Lamb's-quarters
Broadleaf Plantain	Mallow
Buckhorn Plantain	Oxalis
Canada Thistle	Peppergrass
Carpetweed	Pigweed
Chickweed	Purslane
Clover	Ragweed
Cranesbill	Sheep Sorrel
Curly Dock	Shepherd's-purse
Dandelion	Spotted Spurge
Ground Ivy	Speedwell
Heal-all	Yarrow
Henbit	Yellow Rocket
Knotweed	

TABLE 7–4

Broadleaf Weeds Common to the Southern States

Beggarweed	Knotweed
Betony	Lamb's-quarters
Bindweed	Matchweed
Black Medic	Oxalis
Broadleaf Plantain	Peppergrass
Buckhorn Plantain	Prickly Sida
Carpetweed	Prostrate Pigweed
Chickweed	Puncture Vine
Cudweed	Purslane
Curly Dock	Shepherd's-purse
Dandelion	Smartweed
Dichondra	Tropical Chickweed
Heal-all	Yarrow
Henbit	

215. How can I control the dandelions in my lawn when my next-door neighbors let them go in theirs?

Next time you are spreading a weed killer on your lawn, have some left over that you do not want to store until next season. Offer it to your neighbor. Be sure to compliment him or her on how nice the lawn looks later on in the year. When it is time to apply the weed killer again, suggest to your neighbor that you go to the lawn and garden center together and buy some. Try to make it a weekend job when two neighbors get together on a project and have fun doing it. You might even have a barbecue afterward.

216. What is meant by the term noxious weed?

A noxious weed is any plant that has been declared by law to be a harmful or dangerous weed to animals or humans. The list of noxious weeds varies, depending on the state. Some examples of noxious weeds are wild carrot, dodder, giant foxtail, halogeton, marijuana, quackgrass, and annual bluegrass.

217. If I spray 2,4-D to kill the dandelions in my lawn, will it stop any of the dandelion seed from coming up later?

No, 2,4-D kills only those dandelions that are actively growing; it does not have any effect on the seeds in the soil at the time you sprayed your lawn. Killing the actively growing plants will, however, reduce the chances of new plants getting started in your lawn.

Three Reasons Why 2,4-D Will Kill Broadleaf Weeds Without Damaging Mature Lawn Grasses

1. The surface of the leaves are different in the external makeup.
2. The growing habits of the plants are different. Grasses tend to grow upward, whereas broadleaf plants spread out over the ground.
3. The growing point of the plant is located in different places. In grasses it is buried at the base of the plant; on broadleaf plants it is located at the tips of the plant and readily exposed to any chemical treatment.

218. I have seen weed killers at the garden center in several different forms. Which should be used?

Weed killers are usually found in three different forms (formulations): wettable powders, granular, and liquid. Wettable powders (WP) must be mixed in water and require constant stirring to keep the chemical from settling to the bottom of your spray tank. For this reason it is usually best not to buy this form. Your choice between a granular and a liquid weed killer depends on the type of application equipment you own. The granular weed killers can be put on your lawn with a fertilizer spreader. A three-gallon, hand-operated sprayer works well for a liquid formulation. Economically, you will usually get the best buy for your money when you use the liquid weed killers.

219. How can the condition of a lawn affect weeds?

A sparsely covered lawn with large bare spots invites weeds and will quickly become a weed patch if you do not work to remove the weeds. If you have a lawn with dense, healthy turf, chances are you do not have many weeds present.

220. How does mowing of a lawn affect the weeds growing there?

Mowing is one of the most important factors in keeping your lawn weed-free. Mowing too short or removing too much growth in a single clipping will seriously weaken the grass, cause it to be shallow-rooted, and open the door for weed encroachment. If you want to keep your lawn weed-free, it is very important that you know the correct mowing height for the type of grass you have.

221. How soon after my new lawn seed has come up can I spray for weeds?

New grass seedlings are killed easily by herbicides, so you should avoid applying any for as long as possible. A rule of thumb is to wait until you have mowed the grass two to four times before you do any spraying. If the weeds are crowding out the young seedlings, then you may have to spray to save the grass. In this case, cut the recommended application rate in half and apply the chemical twice at a two-day to four-day interval.

222. Should I apply a granular weed killer before or after I water my lawn?

If you are going to apply a granular weed killer, do it *after* you water your lawn. In order for the plants to be killed, the granules must be left in contact with the leaves of the plant. If you wash the granules into the soil, then the weeds will not be killed and you have wasted your money. If your lawn needs watering, do it first, and the water will help the granules stick to the leaves.

223. What is the best way to apply a granular weed killer?

Drop spreaders (gravity flow) are the best applicators to use when applying a granular weed killer. They allow you to get fairly close to the ornamental beds around your lawn, with little chance of damaging the shrubs and flowers. Never use a cyclone spreader unless there is absolutely no chance that you will be near any desirable broadleaf plants.

224. How long does it take for a weed to die after it has been treated with a herbicide?

Usually it takes several days before the plant will die. If you watch the plant closely during this time, you will notice a gradual change in its appearance.

225. When is the best time to control a perennial weed?

The best time is when the plant has been actively growing and using up its stored energy (food) to produce new growth and flowers. Near the end of the growing season is when you will usually get the best results in trying to kill perennial weeds.

226. Can grass seed be sown after a preemergent weed killer has been applied?

This will depend on the type of chemicals used and how long after it has been applied that you wish to seed. Some preemergent chemicals allow you to seed the same day you apply, some require a 60-day waiting period; and others will kill your seedlings up to a year after the chemical was applied. Always read the label carefully to determine how long you will have to wait before you can start seeding your lawn again.

227. How important is it to get even coverage when applying a herbicide?

Uniform coverage is very important when applying chemicals because a concentration of chemicals in one spot could kill the grass. You should always measure the area to be treated to insure that the correct amount of chemical is applied and the coverage is uniform. Remember, underapplication and poor coverage will not give you the desired results, while overapplication will concentrate the chemicals and kill your grass.

228. Why does the label on dicamba (Banvel-D) instruct me not to spray the weeds under the trees in my lawn?

Most postemergent broadleaf weed killers are absorbed and are no longer effective as broadleaf weed killers when they contact the soil. This is not true of dicamba, which moves through the soil and into the plant through the roots. Once it is taken up by the plant, it spreads throughout and usually kills it. This chemical is one you should be extremely careful with when using it around your trees and shrubs.

229. Are there any chemicals available I can use to kill the clumps of grasses growing in my yard?

There are several chemicals on the market that will kill the undesirable bunch grasses (tall fescue, meadow fescue, broomsedge), but they also kill the desirable grasses. The lack of a chemical that will selectively kill the bunch grasses means you either have to spot-treat the clumps or dig them out by hand.

Spot-Killing of Weedy Grasses in Your Lawn

To spot-treat weedy grasses in your lawn, use a kill-all chemical and direct the spray only on those areas where the problem exists. Chemicals to use are dalapon, paraquat, sodium arsenite, cacodylic acid, borax, and amitrol-T.

230. Isn't hand-weeding of dandelions and other broadleaf weeds just as effective as using a chemical spray?

No. Often part of the root, stem, rhizome, or stolon is left in the ground when you dig out a weedy plant. Any of these plant parts is capable of developing into a new plant you will have to remove later. By using a chemical spray, you kill the aboveground portion of the plants as well as the belowground parts.

231. Is there any way to get rid of the weedy grasses growing in my lawn?

You can control the annual grasses (crabgrass, foxtail) without too much trouble by using a preemergent weed killer. The perennial grasses (quackgrass, nimblewill, tall fescue) present a different problem. You can do one of two things to rid your lawn of these pests. Hand-weed or apply a kill-all chemical and resod or seed the areas you treated. Remember, the kill-all chemicals will kill the desirable grasses too, so be careful not to treat any larger areas than absolutely necessary.

232. I have often heard the term monocot and dicot used when some weeds are being discussed. What do these terms mean?

These terms are commonly used by botanists when discussing plants as a convenient way to separate grasses from broadleaf plants. The terms *monocot* (grasses) and *dicot* (broadleaf plants) refer to structures (cotyledons) found on young plants after they have germinated. You have undoubtably noticed that when a grass seed germinates, only a single seedling leaf emerges, while a broadleaf plant has two seedling leaves emerge. Thus the terms *mono-* (one) and *di-* (two).

233. How long can a weed seed stay dormant in the ground before germinating?

Studies have shown some seeds to remain viable for as long as 80 years when buried in soil. Most seeds will remain dormant in the soil for long periods of time until conditions are right for germination.

234. Could you explain why some chemicals kill certain plants without harming others?

It is difficult to give an exact answer. There are many different kinds of plants, and each species varies in its internal and external makeup and the way it reacts to any given chemical. Some plants have, over their leaves, a waxy coating that repels chemicals sprayed on them, making them tolerant to the chemical. The same spray will stick to plants without this waxy coating, allowing the chemical to be absorbed and causing the plant to die. Selectivity of some chemicals is determined within the plant, where it has the ability to convert the chemical into nontoxic forms.

235. Are there any chemicals that I can use to kill the weeds grow-ing in my pond?

There are several excellent chemicals available for weed control in lakes, ponds, and ditches. Before you select one, you need to positively identify the aquatic weeds present. Another important point to consider is where the water is used after it leaves your pond. Any water treated in the pond will carry the chemical with it, and if the water is applied on lawns or crops it could be toxic to them. Read the label on the package containing the chemical before you use it. If your pond is stocked with fish, be sure the chemical you select is nontoxic to fish.

236. I have noticed crabgrass growing in my lawn this fall. Should I try to kill it now or wait until next year?

The best time to control crabgrass is in the spring. Use a pre-emergent chemical when the seeds are just starting to germinate. Once the plant has matured, there are two chemicals (Phenyl Mercuric Acetate, PMA, and Disodium Methyl Arsonate, DSMA) you could spray on the crabgrass to kill it, but usually the best thing to do is just wait until next spring. Both of these chemicals will discolor the turf when applied, especially in hot, dry weather. To be most effective the chemicals should be applied when the crabgrass plants are in the two-leaf to three-leaf stage of growth. Trying to kill it in the fall is not necessary because the first frost will do the job for you. (See map p. 88.)

Crabgrass Control

This pesty lawn weed is a menace to homeowners and their efforts to keep the lawn free of any blemishes. Many a well-mani-cured lawn has seen the invasion of crabgrass ruin its attractive-ness. This need not happen if you understand the life style of a crabgrass plant.

Crabgrass, by definition, is an annual grass, which likes warm weather. For this reason it is referred to as a summer annual. (You will never have to worry about it if you live on a mountain peak in the Rocky Mountains!) The new crabgrass plant starts from seed each spring, after the temperature has warmed the soil. The plant begins inconspicuously at first, but by midsummer it is a full-fledged pest and easy to spot. It's the big clump of light green grass hugging the ground and prolifically producing seedheads. During this stage of its life, crabgrass can be controlled, but it is difficult.

CRAB GRASS GERMINATION ZONES

CRAB GRASS GERMINATION DATES AROUND THE U.S.

June 10 to 20 — April 20-30

June 5 to 15 — April 5 to 15

May 20 to 30 — March 20 to 30

May 5 to 15 — March 5 to 15

Feb. 20 to 28

PREPARED BY THE
RESEARCH DIVISION OF

PAX Company

580 W. 13th So. — Salt Lake City, Utah

At this point you might as well wait and let nature do the job for you. When temperatures start to drop in the fall, the crabgrass plant stops growing and the arrival of frost spells the end of the crabgrass problem for another year.

Well then, how *do* you subdue one of the worst scourges of your lawn? If you'll look at the Crabgrass-Germination Map and locate where you live, you will discover the approximate date to expect crabgrass to make its appearance in your lawn. You must be prepared to act *before* this happens! Go down to the local lawn and garden center and ask for a preemergent crabgrass killer. This is a chemical that will kill crabgrass plants as the seed germinates, never giving it a chance to become established in your lawn. There are all kinds of crabgrass eradicators on the market. All work equally well, so long as you remember one KEY rule. *You must spread it on your lawn before the crabgrass seeds germinate.* If you wait until you see the plant emerge from the soil, you are too late and will have to live with it for another summer. The preemergent chemical works only on the emerging seedling as it is germinating.

What's that? You forgot to put any crabgrass killer on your lawn again and now there is more crabgrass than desired grass. Is there anything you can do about it now? Yes. There are a few chemicals that may be used to get rid of the crabgrass without harming the desired grasses. These postemergent (kills existing plants) chemicals are tricky to use, so be sure to read the directions carefully. Then follow them! Unless your lawn has a really severe case of crabgrassitis, it may be best to live with the problem through the summer and let nature do the work for you. But remember not to be late again next spring with the preemergent chemical because each crabgrass plant produces hundreds of seeds that will compound your problems another year.

237. Is moss a weed?

Moss can be called a weed if it is growing somewhere you do not want it. Usually, raking the soil lightly and then letting it dry out will solve your problem. Moss requires moist conditions to survive so watch your watering schedule and don't keep the soil wet continually. If the soil stays wet for long periods of time, regardless of what you do, then the next step is to put in a drainage system to remove the water from the problem area. Moss grows best in an acid soil, so check the pH of the soil and add lime if necessary to bring the pH to neutral (pH = 7.0).

238. What are some tips on the use and care of a pressurized hand-spray tank?

When using the handspray tank, always keep the pressure low and set the nozzle for coarse droplets. These bigger-sized droplets will be less likely to drift onto nearby desirable plants and cause damage to them. Clean the tank and nozzle of foreign matter before and after each use. This will insure that it is in the best possible working condition and the nozzles won't plug up during use. When you are through with the sprayer, wash it with water; adding one-fourth cup of kitchen ammonia per gallon of water is helpful. This is especially important if you have used a broadleaf weed killer in it and then plan on using the same sprayer to apply an insecticide to your ornamental plants. A trace of 2,4-D left in the tank can kill a very sensitive ornamental plant.

239. Do I need to be concerned with the weather when I am going to apply a herbicide?

Yes. When spraying, pick a day that the temperature is between 55 and 80 degrees and rain is not likely to occur for at least 12 to 18 hours. This gives the chemical a chance to dry on the leaves and to be absorbed by the plant. Remember that 2,4-D is ineffective when washed off into the soil by rain.

240. How can I easily identify a plant that is dying from an application of 2,4-D?

The weed killer 2,4-D is a hormone-type chemical. When applied to a broadleaf plant, it stimulates abnormally fast growth. This accelerated growth causes the leaves to become twisted and curled. The plant literally grows itself to death.

241. Do grasses show different tolerances to weed killers?

Yes, grasses do show different tolerances to weed killers. The use of 2,4-D on an established bluegrass or Bermudagrass lawn will not harm either of them, assuming the recommended rates were used. However, this same chemical used on bentgrass or St. Augustinegrass could be disastrous, resulting in a severe yellowing of the grass to a complete killing of it. Always read the label to be sure the chemical has been tested for use on the type of grass you have in your lawn.

242. How can I control the weeds growing in my dichondra lawn?

The safest way is to hand-pull the weeds if there aren't too many of them. Since dichondra is a broadleaf plant, none of the

broadleaf weed killers can be used on it. Most serious weed problems are caused by plants developing from soil containing an
abundance of inactive weed seeds just waiting for the optimum
conditions before germinating. The best way to keep the weeds
out is to treat the soil with a kill-all chemical (soil sterilant)
before seeding the dichondra.

**243. How can I properly water my lawn to help keep the weeds
out of it?**

Mature, healthy grass will have a deep root system that enables
it to go without water longer than a young weed plant just trying
to get established. With infrequent watering, the surface inch or
two dries out, and the immature weed plants die, whereas the grass
is able to draw moisture from deeper within the soil.

**244. Is it true that knotweed growing in a lawn is an indication
something is wrong with the soil?**

Any time there is knotweed growing in a lawn it is a safe bet that
the soil is severely compacted. Compacted soil weakens the grass,
and once knotweed gets established under these conditions it will
crowd out the desirable grasses. You have to kill the knotweed,
then loosen the soil before seeding or sprigging grass into the
area.

**245. There is a wide-bladed grass growing in my lawn, and the
clumps seem to be spreading more each year. Any idea what it is?**

Chances are that you have a case of tall fescueitis. This perennial grass grows in clumps and will remain a darker green color
than the rest of your lawn in dry weather. Pick a blade of grass
and run your finger carefully down along the edge. If it feels
rough, sort of like a saw blade, then it's probably tall fescue,
provided it is a perennial grass.

**246. How can I rid my lawn of tall fescue after it has invaded my
lawn?**

You have the same problem with this weedy perennial grass that
you do with quackgrass and nimblewill. If you are dealing with a
few clumps, hand-dig them. If the area is too large, then spray
with a nonselective weed killer and resod the area. Your last
choice is to live with it; some people actually prefer it.

**247. It's spring, and I am just starting to put in a new lawn. Is
there any chemical I can use that will not interfere with the germination of my bluegrass seed but will kill the crabgrass seedlings as
they sprout?**

Tupersan (siduron) is one chemical you might want to consider.

When used carefully (instructions must be followed closely), it will give good control of crabgrass while letting the bluegrass grow. It is a good idea to seed a little more heavily than normal (one extra pound of seed per one thousand square feet) to insure a good stand of grass.

What Is the Most Widespread Weed in the World?

In a study of more than five thousand weeds found in the world, the one weed most often found was purple nutsedge, also called nutgrass (*Cyperus rotundus*).

This plant can be easily identified by looking at the stems, which are solid and triangular in shape. The seedheads will be reddish-purple in color.

8

Lawn Diseases

248. How concerned should a homeowner be about a disease ruining the lawn?

Very seldom will a disease ruin a lawn if the homeowner is aware of the damage a disease can do and is prepared to handle the problem. Understanding a few facts about the different diseases and what to do if they develop is usually all that is necessary. Rarely does a disease become severe enough to wipe out an entire lawn.

Three Steps to a Disease-Free Lawn

3. | Apply fungicides.

2. | Use disease-resistant grasses.

1. | Good management practices.

249. What types of organisms are involved in lawn diseases?

The diseases caused by fungi are the primary concern in turfgrass diseases. Bacteria and viruses cause many problems with edible food plants but are of small significance in turfgrasses.

250. What is a fungus?

A fungus is a parasitic form of plant life that is incapable of manufacturing its own food. Some types live on dead organic matter, while others attack living plants. Both can become serious lawn problems. (See Table 8–1.)

251. How many different kinds of fungi attack turfgrasses?

There are well over a hundred different kinds that are all

TABLE 8-1

Typical Life Cycle of a Fungus

Spring	Overwintering spores infect new plant.
Summer	Disease spreads and infects other plants.
Fall	Disease develops in host plant and produces new spores.
Winter	Disease survives as spores in the infected plant and decaying organic matter.

TABLE 8-2

The Fifteen Most Common Lawn Diseases

Common Name	Scientific Name
1. Anthracnose	Colletotrichum graminicola
2. Black Mold	Curvularia species
3. Brown Patch	Rhizoctonia solani
4. Dollar Spot	Sclerotinia homeoecarpa
5. Fairy Rings	Marasmius oreades and other mushrooms
6. Fusarium Blight	Fusarium roseum
7. Gray Leaf Spot	Piricularia grisea
8. Leaf Spot	Helminthosporium species
9. Ophiobolus Patch	Ophiobolus graminis
10. Pink Snow Mold	Fusarium nivale
11. Powdery Mildew	Erysiphe graminis
12. Pythium Blight	Pythium species
13. Red Thread	Corticium fuciforme
14. Rust	Puccinia graminis
15. Slime Molds	Physarium cinereum

adapted to different climatic conditions and grass types. No matter where you live, there will always be some fungus ready to attack your grass, if conditions are favorable.

252. What type of weather favors the growth of fungi?

This depends on the organisms involved. However, they all have a need for moisture. Most fungi do not survive in dry, hot weather. Moisture is essential for rapid development and spreading of a disease. To prevent unnecessary moisture from forming on your lawn, it is best to water in the early morning. This will allow the sun to dry off the moisture, thus inhibiting the spread of disease organisms.

253. At what temperatures do fungi grow best?
From 55 to 80 degrees Fahrenheit is the desirable temperature for fungi growth.

254. What poor lawn-maintenance practices favor disease occurrence?
One is the common practice of keeping the grass wet for long periods of time, thus allowing fungal growth. Another is the use of too much water, along with poor soil drainage and soil compaction, which reduces oxygen in the soil. Other practices such as incorrect fertilizing, mowing too short or too long, and allowing a heavy thatch to accumulate all favor disease buildup in a lawn.

255. Can I try to prevent diseases, or must I wait until they occur?
Once the disease has done its damage and ruined the appearance of your lawn, you will realize the importance of a preventive program. Curative measures may stop the disease, but usually only after some grass has already been destroyed. Application of a fungicide three or four times during the warm periods of the year will usually keep the diseases in check. When in doubt, check with your local lawn and garden center. (See Table 8–3.)

256. What is a broad-spectrum fungicide?
When applied to a lawn, this chemical will control a large number of fungi. It is a shotgun approach, but it's a safe method for the inexperienced person to keep diseases in check on the lawn.

257. Are there any grasses that are resistant to all the different diseases?
No. All grasses have their own diseases to which they are resistant or susceptible. (See Table 8–4.)

258. What are some of the lawn-management practices that help to stop diseases?
Control of diseases starts with selecting a grass that is resistant to diseases. Avoid overfertilization of the grass with nitrogen, aerate the lawn every year, remove shrubs and trees to get good air circulation around the lawn, do not allow thatch to accumulate, and use fungicides.

259. What can be done when a disease is not noticed until some of the grass has started to die?
Usually the disease will not kill the entire plant, and it will recover and fill back in again. To be on the safe side, after you have identified the disease, buy a fungicide and apply at the recommended rates for a curative treatment.

TABLE 8–3

When to Expect Lawn Diseases to Be a Problem

Disease	Bermudagrass Areas	Bluegrass Areas	Pacific Northwest
Brown Patch	Jan., Feb., Nov., Dec.	June, July, Aug., Sept.	July, Aug., Sept.
Dollar Spot	Jan., Feb., March, April, May, Oct., Nov., Dec.	May, June, July, Aug., Sept., Oct.	June, July, Aug., Sept.
Fusarium Blight	—	July, Aug., Sept.	July, Aug., Sept., Oct.
Leaf Spot	year round	March, April, May, Aug.	March, April, May, Sept., Oct.
Pythium Blight	March, April, May, Sept., Oct., Nov.	June, July, Aug.	June, July, Aug.
Red Thread	—	—	April, May, June, Sept., Oct.
Rust	Feb., March, May, Oct., Nov.	July, Aug., Sept., Oct.	June, July, Aug.
Spring Dead Spot	March, April, May	—	—
Stripe Smut	—	April, May, June, Aug.	May, June

TABLE 8-4

The table below lists the common turf diseases and indicates
which grasses are resistant(R) or susceptible(S) to them.

Diseases	Bentgrass	Bermudagrass	Bluegrass	Carpetgrass	Centipedegrass	Chewing Fescue	Red Fescue	Ryegrass	St. Augustine	Tall Fescue	Zoysia
Anthracnose	S	S	S	R	S	R	S	S	R	R	R
Brown Patch	S	S	S	R	S	S	S	S	S	S	S
Dollar Spot	S	S	S	R	S	R	S	R	S	R	S
Fairy Ring	S	S	S	S	S	S	S	S	S	S	S
Fusarium Blight	S	S	S	R	R	S	S	S	R	R	R
Helminthosporium	S	R	S	R	R	R	S	S	R	R	R
Ophilobolus Patch	S	R	S	R	R	R	S	S	R	S	R
Powdery Mildew	R	S	S	R	R	S	S	R	R	R	R
Pythium	S	S	S	R	R	R	S	S	R	R	R
Red Thread	S	R	S	R	R	R	S	S	R	R	R
Rust	S	S	S	R	R	R	S	S	R	S	R
Slime Mold	S	S	S	S	S	S	S	S	S	S	S
Stripe Smut	S	R	S	R	R	R	R	S	R	R	R
Snow Mold	S	R	S	R	R	R	S	S	R	S	R
Spring Dead Spot	R	S	R	R	R	R	R	R	R	R	R

* Different varieties of the individual grasses will show varying degrees of susceptibility and resistance to each disease.

260. Are all the dead spots in my lawn caused by disease?

Chances are that some of the problem spots could be caused by
dog or cat urine, fertilizer burn, improper application of chemicals, drought, burned grass (caused by leaving car mats, boards,
papers, etc., on the grass during hot days), or vandalism.

Dead Spots Are Not Necessarily Caused by Diseases. Consider

1. fertilizer burn,
2. dog or cat urine,
3. poor mowing practices (scalping),

4. compacted soil,
5. misapplication of pesticides,
6. improper watering techniques,
7. insect damage.

261. What is causing the dark-green rings in my yard? Sometimes toadstools will be present.

This is a disease called fairy ring. It is caused by a fungus that develops in the soil and spreads outward in a circular pattern. As the fungus moves outward, the older, dying fungi release the nitrogen they have assimilated from the soil. This release of nitrogen stimulates the growth of the grass, thus causing a dark green ring to show up.

262. Small dead spots, often reddish-purple in color, are appearing on the leaf blades of my grass. Which disease is causing this, and is it serious?

These symptoms appear to be the early stages of helminthosporium leaf spot, which is usually not too serious unless it spreads into the growing points (crown) of the grass. When this happens, the entire lawn may be killed, and the disease is then referred to as Melting or Fading Out.

263. What is the white, soft-looking growth on my grass growing in the shade of the house?

This disease is known as powdery mildew and is usually found in the shade, where the soil is moist. Although the disease is seldom serious, it does distract from the appearance of the lawn. It can be controlled by the use of a fungicide.

264. Why do mushrooms come up in the same place in my lawn every year?

Since mushrooms require a source of decaying wood as a food supply, chances are there was a stump or a piece of wood buried in the lawn during construction. Take a probe and push into the ground; if wood is found, dig it up and the mushrooms will probably disappear.

265. Does thatch have any effect on diseases found in a lawn?

Thatch is one of the major incubating centers for diseases in lawns. Many diseases use the dead leaves and other organic matter as a food source and survive in the thatch because of the higher temperature and moisture. The decaying organic matter absorbs

large amounts of fungicides when they are applied, helping to
protect the fungi from the chemicals.

**266. Are the mushrooms found growing in the outer edges of a
fairy ring edible?**

There are several different kinds of fungi that cause the characteristic "fairy ring"; some of these produce tasty mushrooms
(meadow mushrooms), while others turn out to be the highly
poisonous Death Angel. Unless you really know what you are
doing, I suggest buying your mushrooms at a market.

Folklore of Fairy Rings

Fairy rings are found throughout the world, and the mythology
of their origin has stemmed from the supernatural beliefs of
medieval times. The name *Fairy Ring* is believed to have come
from an ancient superstition explaining the strange green rings as
the pathways formed by dancing fairies, who often stopped their
dancing to rest on the toadstools created by their dancing. Others
thought the rings were the result of children dancing by the moon-
light; when their feet touched the ground, a toadstool was formed.

Down through the years Fairy Rings have always attracted much
attention. Each country—indeed, each village—seemed to have its
own explanation for the cause of the mysterious green rings. In
Holland it was commonly felt that the rings marked the spot where
the devil churned his butter and that one should avoid the rings.
The French would not consider entering one of the rings because
they would be sure to meet a monstrous frog with ugly, bulging
eyes. The English villagers considered the Fairy Rings as good
omens and would build their homes on the land containing them.
Ireland's little people, the leprechauns, were said to have loved to
dance and play games during the late evening hours, and the rings
marked the spot where they had danced.

**267. How do I go about collecting a sample from my diseased
lawn to send to a university for identification?**

Always collect two samples from your lawn, one from the actively growing area of the disease, and another from a nearby spot
where the grass is healthy. Be sure to clearly mark each one so you
don't get them mixed up. Put the samples into a folded piece of
aluminum foil and mail them immediately. Do not add any water
to the samples before placing them in the foil. Send along with the

samples a description of how the disease looks, how long it has been noticeable, fertilization rates used on your lawn, and any other information you think important.

268. My Merion bluegrass lawn has a reddish-brown color to it. What is wrong?

Check the individual leaf blades closely and see if you can find the source of the reddish color; it's probably the fruiting bodies of a disease called *rust*. The disease will disappear when the first frost occurs, but you should be ready for it the next year by keeping the fertility level high and spraying a fungicide at the first sign of rust infection on your grass. Repeat the spray application about 10 days later. Keep an eye on your lawn the rest of the growing season and be prepared to spray again if necessary.

269. Is there any way the disease organisms can be killed in the soil before I plant a new lawn?

Yes. There are a large number of soil fumigants (soil sterilants) available to the homeowner. If the sterilants are used properly, the fungi, as well as nematodes, weed seeds, bacteria, and insects, will be gone from your soil. Be careful when using these chemicals because most of them are very poisonous to humans.

Soil Fumigants for Soil-Disease Control

1. Formaldehyde
2. Chloropicin (tear gas)
3. Methyl Bromide
4. Vapam
5. Mylone
6. Vorlex
7. Nemagon

270. How do diseases spread from one place to another?

Most fungi are reproduced from a structure called a spore (similar to a seed). These spores are so small (if placed end to end, approximately 2,500 of them would equal an inch) that a powerful microscope is needed to see them. Because of their smallness the wind can easily whisk them from one lawn to another (spores have been found 70,000 feet in the air). Diseases can be spread around your lawn by discarded grass clippings, by watering, mowing, and normal foot traffic. Bringing fresh topsoil into your lawn is another excellent way to introduce fungi to your lawn. It has been estimated that one pound of topsoil may have as many as 200 million or more fungi spores in it. Luckily for us, most of them are harmless or beneficial, with only a few being serious plant pests.

271. How can I decide if a disease or some other type of problem has caused the dead spots in my lawn?

Usually, when you have a disease problem, you can pick a few leaf blades out of the infected area and, by examining them closely, see the characteristic symptoms of the disease. Look for any kind of discoloration along the blade edges, circular and oblong, straw-colored, red, or black spots on the blades, shredding or shriveling of the leaves. All these can indicate a disease problem. If dead spots are caused by spilled chemicals or dog urine, the area is usually fairly large and the entire grass plant has died. Very seldom will a disease kill the entire plant, especially in the early stages when you first notice a problem and investigate it. (See Table 8–5.)

272. What single lawn-care technique is my best guard against diseases?

The most important step for you to take in reducing the chance for disease problems is to select a disease-resistant grass when either starting or overseeding your lawn. This will greatly reduce the chances of your ever having to worry about disease infection.

273. The fairy rings in my grass are ruining the looks of my lawn. Is there anything I can do to solve the problem?

Many people enjoy having a few such rings in their lawn because of the green, circular patterns they form and the mysterious stories about them. Since you are not in this group, why don't you fertilize your lawn a little more heavily than you normally do. Be sure the nitrogen content in the fertilizer is high, since you are trying to green-up the rest of your lawn to match that of the fairy rings. Once you mask the fairy rings, the only job left is to get rid of the toadstools by hand-picking them wherever they appear.

274. Just how does a fungus kill a grass plant?

Remember that except in severe cases the entire plant isn't killed but only parts of it are damaged. Usually what happens is the fungus spores land on the grass plant and penetrate the plant. Once inside, the fungus body begins to break down the cells to obtain nutrients and in doing this often secretes toxic chemicals. Often, after the fungi mature, fruiting bodies are formed and can be seen readily on the plant leaves. A good example of this is the

TABLE 8–5

Simple Characteristics to Use in
Identifying Fifteen Common Turf Diseases

Disease	Characteristic
1. Anthracnose	In the late stages of development many black, fruiting bodies will appear on the older grass leaves.
2. Red Thread	Pink to red threadlike structures can be seen growing from the grass leaves.
3. Powdery Mildew	A white cobweb growth will show up on the leaves of the grass blade.
4. Fusarium Blight	The grass will usually die in a ringlike pattern, 4 to 8 inches in diameter, with a tuft of the grass surviving in the center.
5. Leaf Spot	Lesions (dead spots) will occur on all visible parts of the plant. The spots will be yellow with a dark border around them. The entire plant may turn yellow and die if the disease is serious enough.
6. Fairy Rings	Dark-green circles, 2 to 100 feet in diameter will appear. The fruiting bodies, toadstools, will develop from the dark-green areas when there is sufficient moisture in the soil.
7. Ophiobolus Patch (Frog-Eye)	A patch of grass 1 to 3 feet will die, leaving a light-yellow-to-bronze appearance in the turf. The grass that was killed will not grow back, and weeds or resistant grasses will fill in the center, leaving dead grass exposed on the edge.
8. Slime Mold	White-to-grayish-colored growth will cover the grass plants in small patches. When dry, the color of the organism changes to a grayish-black, and, if crushed, a grayish powder will be present. If looked at closely, the individual organisms will look like a small white ball with a black spot on it.
9. Rust	Reddish-brown to orange pustules form on the leaves and stems of the grass. As the disease

spreads, it will move up and down the leaves along the veins, and parallel rust-colored patterns will form.

10. Pythium — Often in the early morning, if the humidity is high, a white, cottony growth can be seen on the grass. When the sun comes out and dries the grass, the cottony mass disappears. A dark-green, greasy-looking spot, 1 to 2 inches in diameter, will appear, followed by the grass's turning yellow and dying.

11. Brown Patch — "Smoke rings," ½ to 2 inches wide, may border the infected area. These grayish rings around the circumference of the disease will occur in early mornings when the humidity is high. Inside the rings the grass will first turn a purplish color, then brown as it dies.

12. Dollar Spot — On humid mornings a cottony mass the size of a silver dollar may be seen. The individual areas on a leaf will die, turning a tan color with a reddish band at each end of the dead area.

13. Snow Mold — Usually seen at the edge or under snow as a whitish growth that will turn gray upon drying. After the leaves of the grass turn brown, small, black, fruiting bodies can be seen embedded in the leaves.

14. Spring Dead Spot — Circular spots of grass are dead when the Bermudagrass comes out of its winter dormancy. These areas may be 3 to 5 feet in diameter and cover entire lawns. The exact fungus causing the disease has not been identified.

15. Stripe Smut — First symptoms to occur are long green stripes on the leaf blade. As the disease matures, the stripes turn black, and a black powdery material will escape when the plants are brushed. The leaves usually split and curl up as the disease reaches the final stages.

rust disease (*Puccinia graminis*). In this stage the damage is already done, but those fruiting bodies do contain the spores that insure another year of disease problems.

275. *How safe are fungicides?*

This depends on whether you are a grass plant, fungus, or a homeowner. If a fungicide is applied according to the information given on the label, the chances of damaging the grass are not too great. About the only way you can burn the grass with a fungicide is to apply it in extremely hot weather (above 85 degrees). Be careful not to get any of the fungicide on you because most of these chemicals are poisonous. Always wash with soap and water immediately after using any fungicide.

276. *Will grass plants germinating from seed be resistant to diseases if the seed has been treated with a special seed-fungicide?*

No. The purpose of treating the seed with a fungicide is to prevent a disease known as damping-off from killing the young seedlings shortly after they have germinated. This disease will very seldom attack older plants. Resistance to diseases is a genetic characteristic in plants, and the treatment of the grass seed will not make the germinating plant more resistant to the multitude of disease organisms that might someday try to infect it.

277. *Will heavy fertilization prevent diseases from infecting my lawn?*

No. The best fertilization program is one that applies the nutrients in the proper proportions to the plant's needs. The two main nutrients you are really concerned with are nitrogen and potassium. High nitrogen levels in the soil cause the plants to be very susceptible to diseases such as leaf spot, brown patch, and gray-leaf spot. Low nitrogen levels favor red thread, dollar spot, and rust. Follow the recommended rates of nitrogen fertilization for the grass in your lawn, and you should not have too many difficulties. High potassium levels seem to reduce the occurrence of certain diseases, such as leaf spot, brown patch, red thread, dollar spot, and Fusarium blight.

278. *Can I mix my fungicide with an insecticide so I have to spray the lawn only once?*

Certain fungicides and insecticides can be mixed together safely. Often this information is not included on the label of the chemicals. You will have to write the manufacturers or check at the garden center to get this information. Do not mix two chemicals together unless you have checked to be sure it is safe to do so; the results could be disastrous to the grass. You would be better off to take the time and apply them separately.

279. *Are all diseases caused by some kind of living creatures?*

Turf diseases can be categorized under two general headings: infectious (bacterial, fungal, nematodes, viruses), and noninfectious diseases. The noninfectious diseases are the result of mechanical damage, genetic defects, improper balance of nutrients, and unfavorable climatic conditions.

280. What is a systemic fungicide?

A systemic fungicide is taken into the plant primarily through the roots and dispersed throughout, giving it a built-in defense against fungi. The big benefit in using this kind of fungicide is that the entire plant is protected for long periods of time. Many of the newer fungicides being developed belong in this classification.

A conventional fungicide sprayed on the leaves does not always cover the entire plant, thus allowing the fungi a chance to infect the plants. These types of fungicides are also washed off the plants when it rains or when you water.

281. Do lawn diseases occur only under hot, humid weather conditions?

No. Usually diseases are most active during the hot, humid weather, but some, such as snow mold, do best in the cold, damp weather when the snows are melting away. Dollar spot and red thread like damp, cool days to damage your lawn. There is no steadfast rule about what the weather conditions must be before a disease attack can occur.

282. I live in the West, where we seem to have fewer problems with diseases than homeowners do who live in the Midwest and South. Why is this so?

Many of the diseases are present in all parts of the United States, but, unless the climate is conducive to disease growth, they remain dormant. One of the most important factors needed in order for a fungus to develop is a moist condition for a continued length of time. Fungi have a rough time getting started if the humidity is always low, as it is in the desert.

Guide to When Lawn Diseases Might Become a Problem

If TEMPERATURE plus HUMIDITY = 180 or higher, then be on the lookout for disease problems in your lawn.

EXAMPLES: 97 degrees F. + 95% = 192 . . . . good chance of a disease problem

65 degrees F. + 75% = 140 . . . . poor chance of a disease problem

9

Insects and Their Control

The use of chemical insecticides to control insects deserves a special introduction. These materials are toxic to man and animals, as well as to insects. And the affect on the environment must also be taken into account.

For years a controversy has been raging over the use of these chemicals. In many cases, facts have given way to emotional pleas, and some excellent insecticides have been taken off the market. One fact is known: there has never been a death caused by an insecticide when it was used according to the instructions on the label.

The United States Department of Agriculture conducted a study of deaths caused by pesticides in the three-year period from 1963 to 1966. The results were astounding! During this time, there were 62 pesticide-related deaths; 65 percent of the victims were six years old or younger. More recent reports place the figure at 70 percent and lower the age to five years or younger.

What caused a majority of these 62 deaths? Thirty-three percent were attributed to failure to read or follow the label directions. Twenty-six percent could be narrowed down to improper storage of the chemicals. Transferring the chemicals to an unmarked container led to 21 percent of the deaths. Failure to wear the proper clothing when using these chemicals accounted for 16 percent. Thirteen percent of the deaths were caused by spilling the chemicals on clothes or skin. Improper disposal of chemical containers accounted for 11 percent. The final 5 percent was caused by contaminated water supplies or drifting of materials during application. Many of the 62 deaths involved one or more of these reasons, and this is why the total percent is greater than one hundred.

The emotional response after seeing these figures is to halt the use of all insecticides and pesticides in general. This type of reaction should not be allowed to govern the total use of these chemicals. When properly used, insecticides are a valuable garden tool that can help to improve living conditions. Without the use of insecticides, you would still be looking for a worm in every apple you ate. Your lawn, garden, and flowers would never be as beautiful as they are today without the control of insects that stand ready to destroy them.

I am not advocating the indiscriminate use of chemicals for the control of insects. Nor am I in favor of emotionally sponsored laws regulating the use of insecticides. These chemicals are important to have available for your use around the home. If you use them properly, you will not become a government statistic in a pesticide-fatality study.

In October 1972 Congress passed a law to govern the use of pesticides. The primary purpose of its enactment was to protect you, the consumer, from misusing pesticides and harming yourself or someone else. The branch of the government responsible for enforcing the law is the Environmental Protection Agency (EPA). Every pesticide has to be registered with EPA, and so you are guaranteed a safe product that will do the job effectively if you follow the label directions.

EPA has the authority to levy a fine on any consumer who misuses a pesticide. The misuse of chemicals endangers our environment and every living thing on earth. Common sense then suggests that we all need to be careful. No one wants to be responsible for a pesticide accident or an environmental problem. The best way to avoid a mistake is to always read and follow the label directions.

PROS AND CONS OF USING INSECTICIDES

There are four general categories of potential hazards: 1. Some of the chemicals are long lasting and persist in nature for years, polluting the air, water, and soil. This problem usually occurs only when the chemicals have been applied carelessly and in excessive amounts. The long-lasting residual of DDT, chlordane, dieldrin, aldrin, and heptachlor are the primary reasons EPA removed these chemicals from the garden centers. 2. Many of the chemicals are not selective in the pests they kill. Beneficial as well as harmful insects become victims. 3. Wildlife is often another innocent victim of improper use of insecticides. 4. Last, but certainly not the least important, is the harm these chemicals can cause to humans. Every chemical is poisonous and should be handled carefully.

The bad side of the story always seems to be the one receiving all the publicity, but there is a good side of interest to you. Primarily, the benefits from the use of chemicals for insect control revolve around the protection of humans and animals from diseases and bothersome pests in the yard and home.

Diseases such as malaria and typhus have pretty well been brought under control with the use of insecticides, saving thousands of lives every year. Home gardeners and lawnskeepers can easily protect their lawns and shrubs from damage caused by insects. The farm communities of the United States rely heavily on the use of insecticides to protect their crops, thereby producing a surplus of food each year. The proper use of insecticides has led us down a prosperous path since the end of World War II. Without these chemicals our outdoor living would not be as enjoyable as it is today.

Getting back to lawn care and the use of insecticides in the yard, let's briefly touch upon how I have approached the subject of insecticides and which ones you should consider using. As previously mentioned, the Environmental Protection Agency is responsible for regulating the use of insecticides. If this government agency decides a certain chemical is too hazardous, it will have the chemical removed from the market. If, after additional information on the chemical is gathered, showing it safe for consumer use, EPA can reinstate the insecticide, and it will be returned to the retail market.

Because of the possibility of some insecticides being removed and then later brought back to the counter for sale, I have gone ahead and listed various insecticides in this chapter. Keep in mind that some may not be available, due to an EPA decision, so you may have to select an alternate from the suggested insecticides.

My favorite insecticide is one called diazinon, a phosphate chemical that kills a broad spectrum of insects but has a short life in nature. It readily breaks down and does not cause a residual or build-up in plants, animals, or the soil when applied according to the instructions found on the label.

There are more than 5,000 different insecticides, based on about 70 basic formulas, from which you can choose. I have not attempted to list all of them for you. If you're in doubt about which chemical to use, your best source of information is your local state cooperative extension office or the nearest branch of the United States Agriculture Department. Both can be found listed in your telephone directory.

When getting ready to buy an insecticide, remember that 70 percent of pesticide deaths are children under five years of age. Don't you become responsible for one of these deaths by your own carelessness!

283. What does the term insecticide mean?
An insecticide is any chemical that is used to kill insects.

284. What are contact, stomach, and systemic insecticides?
These terms refer to the way in which the chemicals kill the insects. Contact insecticides kill the insects upon spraying. The stomach insecticides are sprayed on the plants and kill the insects when they eat the plant. Systemic insecticides are taken into the plant and kill the insects that suck or rasp the juices from the plants.

285. What are some of the different ways an insecticide can be applied?
Insecticides can be purchased in four common forms: dusts, sprays, granules, and aerosol cans. The areas to be covered and the availability of the chemical in the form you prefer will determine which method is used for application. Usually the granular insecticides are the most economical to apply.

286. How dangerous are insecticides to the person applying them?
The first rule to follow when using any chemical is to read the label carefully two or three times. Having done this, you will know how potentially dangerous the chemical is and what precautions to take to protect yourself. All chemicals should be handled very carefully. Anytime a chemical comes in contact with your skin, wash the chemical off immediately with hot soapy water. (See Table 9–1.)

287. What are some general precautions to follow when using insecticides?

TABLE 9-1

Relative Toxicity of Different Insecticides

High	*Med.*	*Low*
Di-Syston	Diazinon	Allethrin
Ethion	Karathane	Aramite
Lead Arsenate	Lindane	Malathion
Nicotine	Rotenone	Methoxychlor
Parathion		Pyrethrins
Phorate		Ryania
Systox		Sabadilla
TEPP		Sevin
Toxaphene		Sulfur

a. Read the label carefully. Understanding the chemical you are using could be a matter of life and death.

b. Keep all chemicals out of the reach of children.

c. Cover food when treating areas around the house.

d. If any chemicals are spilled on the skin, wash the area immediately with hot, soapy water.

e. Do not smoke while applying chemicals.

f. Never put chemicals into unmarked containers.

288. I have heard that insecticides and fungicides must not be mixed together for application. Is this correct?

You must be extremely careful in mixing different chemicals because drastic results could occur. Unless the label gives directions, it is best not to mix chemicals. Often when two chemicals are mixed, their activity is changed, and the results could be very unexpected and disastrous.

289. Do insects help get rid of thatch from a lawn by using it as food?

In most cases the insects will not use the accumulated thatch as food, since it consists of dead and decaying material. Insects like the nice, green grass for their meals. The thatch does act as a home for the insects where they can breed, sleep, and hide from unsuspecting eyes. Thatch breeds trouble for homeowners.

290. What is a nematode?

It is a microscopic, worm-like animal that lives in the soil and feeds on the roots of plants. The damage done by nematodes is often mistaken as a disease problem or grub damage. There are several chemicals on the market that will kill nematodes, but, as mentioned, it is often impossible to diagnose the problem.

291. *How serious a problem are nematodes in lawns and gardens?*

Very seldom will nematodes completely kill the grass in your lawn. They usually cause the grass plants to be stunted in size and yellowish in color. Nematodes can do considerable damage to various garden plants, but in most cases the damage done to lawns is not too critical.

292. *What chemicals can be used to control nematodes?*

There are several different chemicals available. Check with your local lawn and garden center for advice on which to use. Some of the more common ones are Nemagon (DD), Vapam, Mylone, and methyl bromide.

293. *Is there a chemical available for the control of earthworms?*

Before chlordane was taken off the market, it was used successfully for earthworm control. Presently there is not a chemical on the market that is labeled for use in killing earthworms.

294. *What does the sod webworm look like, and how does it damage the grass?*

The best way to describe the sod webworm moth is to compare it to a small, hand-rolled cigarette. When the moth is not in flight, the wings fold into tubular form. The moth is usually one half to three fourths of an inch long and is seen most often at night as it flies erratically over the lawn. The moth does not harm the grass, but the larva (young wormlike stage of growth) is the villain. It chews the grass blades off at ground level and causes the grass to appear as if clipped unevenly.

295. *A white, wormlike insect with a brown head and curved body is eating the roots of my grass. What is it?*

This sounds like an infestation by white grubs. They can become very serious if allowed to get out of control. If there are five to six grubs per square foot, immediate control measures must be taken.

296. *What are the major turf insects that cause problems to homeowners?*

Those insect pests that are the most bothersome are webworms, chiggers, grubs, mole crickets, chinchbugs, spidermites, armyworms, ants, cutworms, and fleas. Some of these insects do not damage the lawn but are a major nuisance to the homeowner.

Lawn Pests and Damage They Do

FEED ON PLANT ROOTS

grubs	wireworms
ants	pillbugs
crickets	earthworms

FEED ON PLANT STEMS AND LEAVES

sod webworm	lucerne moth
armyworms	grasshopper
cutworms	leaf bug

FEED BY SUCKING PLANT JUICES

chinch bug	spittlebug
false chinch bug	mites
leafhopper	scale insects

BOTHERSOME PESTS
(Do not damage plants)

earwigs	millipedes
ticks	centipedes
chiggers	slugs
thrips	spiders
fleas	snails

Want to Know If Chinch Bugs Are Your Problem?

Use this quick test to find out.

Step 1. Cut both ends out of a 6-inch-diameter tin can.

Step 2. Push the tin can ¾ of the way into the ground.

Step 3. Fill the tin can up with water for 10 to 15 minutes.

Step 4. Check for chinch bugs after 10 to 15 minutes. If they are present, they will float to the surface.

Are Slugs a Problem in Your Lawn?

The best chemical on the market that is effective in killing slugs is Mesurol. It is used as a bait and will rid your lawn of those slimy pests.

297. Is there any specific time of year that an insecticide should not be applied?

The only time that can definitely be given is when the ground is frozen. At this time most insects should be gone, and, of course, the frozen ground cannot absorb the chemical, which could easily be washed into nearby streams and ponds. By a careful reading of the label, you will find enough information to know when to apply the chemical.

298. Why do gardeners refer to the small, brown moth so often seen flitting around lawns as the sod webworm?

The damage is done to the grass plant while this insect is in the infant (worm) stage of growth; hence the interest in the worm stage. Most insects go through several stages of development from infancy to adulthood. The adults (moths) do very little damage to the grass, but their contribution of eggs insures a new generation of insects the following year.

299. I applied an insecticide to my lawn, and three days later I noticed some insects were not even bothered. Why?

Many insects have formed an immunity to certain insecticides. You may need to try a different type of chemical. Another possibility is that the insecticide you are using simply does not have the ability to kill the insects giving you the problems. Check the label and see which insects are listed as being susceptible to the chemical you are applying. A third possibility is that your lawn is vigorously growing, and the insects are thriving on the new plant growth that does not have any of the insecticides on it.

300. Why is it you can kill certain insects and in a few days more they are back again?

First, if your neighbor doesn't apply any insecticides, insects from his lawn will move into yours after your spray wears off. The life cycle of some insects is so short that you can kill the adults and in just a few days a new generation of insects has hatched and reinfested your lawn and garden.

301. I am thinking about using a poisonous bait to control the rodents damaging my lawn. What are some of the ingredients in poisonous baits, and is there any danger involved when using them?

The more common poisonous baits are made of arsenic or strychnine or a combination of the two. As you probably already know, both of these chemicals can be fatal if eaten by humans or pets. If you use poisonous baits, be sure they are kept in a marked container and out of the reach of children.

TABLE 9-2

Lawn Pests and Insecticides Used to Control Them

	Grubs	Ants	Sod Webworms	Wireworms	Chinch Bugs	Armyworms	Cutworms	Chiggers	Leafhoppers
Baygon*	S	S	S						
Dursban*		S	S		S				
Dylox*	S		S						
Diazinon	S	S	S	S	S	R	R	R	S
Lindane	R	R	R	R	R	R	R	S	S
Malathion	R	R	R	R	R	R	R	S	S
Proxol*						S	S		
Sevin	R	S	S	R	S	S	S	R	S
Toxaphene	S	S	R	R	R	R	R	S	R

S = susceptible

R = resistant

* Labeled for use in controlling these insects only.

302. **Why is there always a flock of birds pecking around in my lawn?**

This is a good indication you have an insect problem you are not yet aware of. These birds are pecking and digging up soil-borne insects. Investigate and get rid of these insects as soon as possible.

303. **Some moths and butterflies are very pretty, yet I am told that in different stages of their life they are very destructive to plants. Would you briefly explain the different stages of growth of a moth or butterfly and tell which stage is most destructive?**

Most insects go through four different stages in their life cycle: 1. egg; 2. larva (caterpillar); 3. pupa (cocoon); and 4. the adult (moth). In most cases it is the enormous appetite in the larva stage that does the most damage. The adults, although not directly responsible for plant damage, may be considered even more destructive because they are responsible for laying eggs and giving new life to their species.

304. The label on the insecticide I purchased does not say how long the chemical will be good after I open it. Is there a general rule on the shelf life of chemicals?

If the chemicals are stored in a dry place and are not allowed to freeze during cold weather, they are generally good for one year, two years at the most. Always try to buy the amount of chemical you will need and use it up in one season. This way you won't have to worry about shelf life or inquisitive children!

305. Of the different ways you can buy insecticides, which formulation is least likely to deteriorate with age?

Those chemicals coming in aerosol cans usually will have the longest shelf life. The chemical in these cans is usually good until the can is empty.

306. How many different kinds of insects are there in the world?

The exact answer to this question is not known. Every year more and more new insects are identified. Somewhere in the neighborhood of over a million various kinds of insects would be a good estimate. The beetles comprise about 40 percent of the total, while moths, butterflies, wasps, bees, and ants account for another 35 percent.

Astonishing Facts About the Insect Population Explosion

It has been estimated that at least 80 percent of all the animal life on the earth is made up of insects. Over a million different insect species have been identified, and the number is still increasing. Some researchers estimated that there could be as many as three billion (3,000,000,000) insects living on each square mile of land. Compare this to the present world population, slightly less than three billion people, and you can quickly see the insect population explosion is something we don't want to get out of control.

307. How many different kinds of insects are actually harmful to plants?

Considering the large number of different kinds of insects, the ones that are harmful to plants are nominal. Approximately 1 percent of all the known insects damage plants. Only a very small fraction of this number is harmful to turfgrasses.

308. I read a newspaper article that was discussing the toxicity of different insecticides. In the article the symbols $LD_{50} = 12$, $LD_{50} = 280$, and $LD_{50} = 5,000$ were used. What do they refer to?

Each insecticide on the market today has gone through years of research before it was made available for consumer use. One of the research tests involves feeding various amounts of the insecticide to rats to determine how poisonous the chemical is. The letters LD (lethal dose)$_{50}$ are part of a poison-rating system that indicates how much of the insecticide being tested must be orally fed to the rats to kill 50 percent of the test group. The numerals 12, 280, and 5,000 are numerical comparisons of the different insecticides that tell you how dangerous the insecticides are. The smaller the number, the more poisonous the insecticide.

309. What should I do with an insecticide container when it is empty?

It is important to dispose of these containers in a place where wildlife, livestock, or people will not come in contact with them. The contamination of local water supplies should also be avoided. If your city has a land-fill garbage dump, then the containers can be disposed of in the garbage. Another solution is to bury the containers deeply in the ground if you are in a location where it is convenient to do this.

310. What are some of the careless things people do with insecticides that could lead to their death or someone else's?

There are four major reasons for the deaths of careless people who use insecticides incorrectly. These are (1) failure to read the label; (2) storage of chemicals where children can reach them; (3) improper disposal of empty containers; and (4) putting insecticides in unmarked containers, especially pop bottles and milk cartons.

311. What symptoms will I have if I am poisoned by an insecticide?

A definite answer to this question is not possible. Different chemicals cause different types of symptoms to appear. The symptoms can vary according to the concentration of the chemical, how it entered the body, the weight and age of the person, and even according to the sex of the individual. Whenever you use an insecticide, you should be aware of the dangers involved to yourself, so that you can be on the lookout for any sudden changes in your health. Some signs or symptoms to be on the lookout for are headaches, weakness, nausea, impaired vision (blurring), diarrhea, chest pains, and vomiting. These symptoms may occur immediately or several hours after exposure to a chemical.

312. When I have spilled an insecticide on my skin, how long can I safely wait before washing it off?

This will depend on the chemical you are using. I, personally, would wash it off immediately, regardless of the chemical. Prolonged contact with the skin increases the amount of chemical absorbed by your body. Washing the chemical off within the first five minutes is usually pretty effective, but if you wait for as long as thirty minutes, then the washing is not as effective. After applying an insecticide, be sure to wash your hands thoroughly before eating any food.

313. How do the deaths from the misuse of pesticides compare to accidental deaths in the United States?

The actual number of deaths each year due to pesticide poisoning is difficult to accurately determine. Present reports place the figure between 20 and 50 pesticide-related deaths per year. Deaths caused by the misue of pesticides prove to be nominal in comparison with accidental deaths due to automobiles (60,000), drownings (1,707), or poisons other than pesticides (420).

Ten-year Survey Showing Deaths Due to Insect Bites and Venomous Creatures

Type of Insect or Creature	Number of Deaths
Spider bites	27
Scorpion stings	6
Tick paralysis	8
Bee, Wasp, Ants	60
Snakebites	48

314. I had finished spraying an insecticide on my lawn, and a little chemical was left over so I sprayed it on my flowerbeds. Two days later the flowers and leaves were curling up and turning black. The label on the container said it was safe to use the chemical on the flowers. What went wrong?

This is a difficult question to answer without additional information. From the description of the dying flowers I would say 2,4-D could be the culprit. If you used any 2,4-D recently in your sprayer to kill weeds in your lawn, then I could be sure of the cause. Any time you use 2,4-D, you should thoroughly wash out your sprayer. Very sensitive flowers are easily killed even after a spray can that has had 2,4-D in it has been rinsed out several times. To be on the safe side, never use the same sprayer to apply 2,4-D and insecticides to your lawn and flowers.

315. *Is it important to know the living habits of the insects that I want to kill?*

Yes. If the insect lives in the ground, you have to apply the chemical and wash it into the soil, where it comes in contact with the pest. If the insect lives aboveground, then you want to spray the plant surfaces and let the chemical dry on the leaves, so that when the insect lands on the plant or eats the leaves, the chemical is ready to do its job. By understanding the insect's living habits, you have a better chance of getting rid of it by applying the chemicals properly.

316. *What are broad-spectrum insecticides?*

These are chemicals that kill a wide range of insects found in lawns. They're the best kind for a homeowner to use.

317. *What are some advantages to using a broad-spectrum insecticide?*

Most homeowners do not have the background to identify all insects and then select a specific chemical to get rid of each one. The advantage in using a broad-spectrum insecticide is that the homeowner can apply it once and kill several different kinds of insects.

318. *What should I look for in a granular insecticide when it is to be applied by a drop-spreader?*

For the best coverage of your lawn, the granules should be uniform in size and should flow freely through the holes in the spreader.

319. *What precautions should I be aware of while applying a granular insecticide with a drop-spreader?*

The way you spread the insecticide should be given some thought. If you apply it by going in opposite directions (parallel rows), be sure you have a slight (one to two inches) overlap in your patterns. This will insure that all your lawn is treated. In large, open areas a circular pattern may be used if it is more convenient. Always shut the hopper whenever you have to stop because of an obstacle or when you come across an area you've already treated. This will prevent overtreating areas and possibly damaging the grass. Areas you cannot reach with the spreader can be treated by spreading the granules by hand or by a homemade shaker (holes drilled in the lid of a jar). Try to get the same coverage you are getting with your drop-spreader.

320. *How often should I spray my lawn to keep the insects from becoming a problem?*

This will vary, but usually two to three times a season will keep most of the insects from becoming a problem in your lawn. If a build-up of insects is noticed during the year, an occasional extra spraying may be necessary.

10

Maintenance Tips

321. What can be done to get the grass to grow better in the heavy shade under maple and oak trees?

Three basic things can be done to help keep a stand of grass in heavy shade. Lower-tree branches should be pruned 10 to 15 feet up from the ground, and the upper part of the tree should have some of the limbs selectively removed to allow more light to penetrate to the grass below. Tree roots at the surface of the ground rob the grass of the nutrients. Therefore, either follow a good fertilizer program, or bring in 5 to 7 inches of topsoil to put over the top of the roots; then plant grass seed. In most cases the grass will continue to thin-out in heavy shade, so plan on reseeding every year to maintain cover under the trees.

322. How can I keep the grass from spreading into my flower beds?

The best method is to install metal or plastic grass barriers along the edge of the flowerbeds. The barrier should be buried at least four inches into the ground with just enough exposed aboveground to prevent the grass from growing over the top into the flowerbeds. Be sure that the metal exposed above the ground does not have any sharp or jagged edges. The metal strip should not stick out of the ground too high because the blade of your lawn mower could hit it and be damaged. (See fig. 10–1.)

323. Is rolling a lawn ever harmful?

Yes. If the ground is too wet, the soil can be severely compacted, and grass roots will find it difficult to obtain oxygen, thus weakening the entire grass plant.

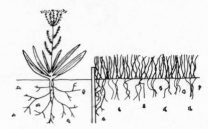

Figure 10–1. Metal or plastic barriers prevent grass from spreading into flowerbeds.

324. What are some of the reasons for rolling a lawn?

Rolling a lawn helps firm-up the soil and push the grass crowns (growing point of grass) down into the soil, where there is less chance for them to dry out in hot weather. If the rolling is done after seeding, it helps push the seed into better soil contact and improves the chances for good seed germination. If a person is careful and waits for the soil to be in the right condition, rolling can be used to help level a lawn if followed by an aerification program.

325. When should I roll my lawn?

In the Northern part of the United States, where the ground freezes for part of the year, the best time to roll a lawn is in the early spring, just after the ground has thawed. In the areas where the ground does not freeze, the lawns should be rolled soon after the grass has begun actively growing. You should not roll a lawn more than once a year.

326. How important is it to have good soil drainage in my lawn?

This is one aspect of lawn care that is very important and is often overlooked. If there is poor drainage in a lawn, the ground will become very wet and soggy for long periods of time. This means that adequate oxygen will not be supplied to the plant through the roots, causing the grass to become shallow-rooted and to tear up easily.

327. What causes moss to grow in my lawn, and how can I get rid of it?

Moss will usually be found anywhere the grass is not thick enough and the soil is too moist for long periods of time. This condition will occur most often in heavy shade, but, if a soil is poorly drained, moss will grow in full sunlight.

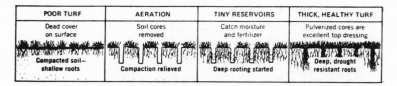

POOR TURF	AERATION	TINY RESERVOIRS	THICK, HEALTHY TURF
Dead cover on surface	Soil cores removed	Catch moisture and fertilizer	Pulverized cores are excellent top dressing
Compacted soil— shallow roots	Compaction relieved	Deep rooting started	Deep, drought resistant roots

Figure 10–2. Aeration keeps turf soft and springy and helps to build healthy root structure. *Drawings courtesy of Ryan Equipment Co., Lincoln, Nebraska, © 1973.*

328. What is meant by aerifying a lawn?

The removal of small soil plugs from a lawn, known as aerifying, improves air movement in the grass-root zone. It can be done by machine and is very beneficial to lawns when done properly. (See fig. 10–2.)

329. What are some of the benefits gained from aerifying a lawn?

a. Increases the exchange of oxygen between the soil and roots.

b. Stimulates new and faster growth of the grass plants.

c. Helps to level a lawn if the cores are shredded and dragged into the low spots.

d. Reduces soil compaction.

e. Reduces disease and insect problems by helping to get rid of unwanted thatch.

f. Can help prepare a seedbed when overseeding into an established lawn.

330. How often should a lawn be aerified?

Once or twice a year is adequate for most lawns. Aerification is a lot of work and not always necessary, but the end results are usually worth the effort. The aerification process leaves the lawn looking poorly for a week or two before the grass fully recovers.

331. When overseeding and aerification are both planned, which should be done first?

By all means overseed the lawn first, then aerify. This allows the soil cores to be brought up on the surface of the grass to cover the seed. Much of the seed will end up in the aerification holes, and this seed will usually be the first to germinate.

332. What does the term thatch refer to in a lawn?

Thatch is a term used to describe the accumulation of organic matter (dead grass leaves, roots, and stems) in a layer on the

Figure 10–3. Thatch inhibits the growth of thick, healthy roots.

surface of the soil. Allowing tree leaves to be mulched by chopping them up when mowing will aid in the rapid build-up of a thatch in your lawn.

Expect thatch to be a problem if you have any of the following grass varieties in your lawn:

Bentgrass,
Bermudagrass,
Centipedegrass,
Improved bluegrasses,
St. Augustinegrass, or
Zoysia.

333. In what way is thatch harmful to a lawn?

The layering of organic matter prevents oxygen from being able to diffuse into the rootzone, causing the grass to be very shallow-rooted and easily torn out. Thatch is an excellent breeding ground for harmful insects and disease organisms. Because water will not readily soak through a thatch layer, it runs off and is wasted, along with any fertilizer it has dissolved. (See fig. 10–3.)

334. Is it necessary to dethatch a lawn if it is aerated every year?

Unless the grass is allowed to become extremely long between mowings, aerification once a year will usually make it unnecessary to remove thatch from a lawn.

335. When is the best time to dethatch a lawn?

The early spring or late fall (when the grass is not actively growing) is the best time for dethatching. Be prepared to bring up several bushels of dead grass during the process.

336. What do the words soil texture mean?

This is a term coined by the agronomists for the amount of sand, silt, and clay in a soil. Each of the three particles is measured in a soil sample and expressed as a percentage of the total. These percentages are used to determine the texture of a soil. Only a slight change in the percentages of the three particles will affect the determination of the soil texture. (See Table 10–1.)

337. How important is it for me to know the texture of a soil?

Every year many homeowners buy "topsoil" for around their homes and find out later that nothing will grow in it. Chances are they were sold a "subsoil," which usually is higher in clay content and rather difficult for growing good grass. Anyone who understands soil texture would know that any soil that has more than 30–35 percent clay will probably cause problems. Soils this high in

TABLE 10–1

% Clay	% Silt	% Sand	Soil Texture
15	40	45	loam
20	20	60	sandy loam
20	60	20	silt loam
30	55	15	silty clay loam
35	35	30	clay loam
40	20	40	clay loam
45	50	5	silty clay
55	30	15	clay

clay tend to compact readily, thus robbing the grass roots of the much-needed oxygen.

338. Is it possible to have a good lawn when the soil is poor?

Yes, if extra care is taken in maintaining everything else in tiptop shape. This means watering at the correct times, mowing high rather than short, fertilizing frequently, and maybe aerifying every year to reduce soil compaction.

339. Does a soil test tell you anything useful?

Yes, but if you have a soil test done on your lawn and do not pay attention to the results, it is of no value to you. If you heed the results and use them to improve the maintenance of your lawn, then you will probably be rewarded with one of the best lawns in the neighborhood.

340. What can be done in areas where the grass was killed by spilled gasoline or oil?

In small areas where only small amounts of gas or oil are in-

volved, the soil can be removed six to eight inches deep and replaced. If the areas are very large and heavily soaked, then it will
be very expensive to remove the soil and bring in fresh topsoil. In
this case, a decorative mulch, such as redwood bark, crushed red
brick, or white stone, can be spread over the damaged areas.

341. What does the term pH mean?

The term *pH* is used to designate the concentration of hydrogen
ions in a soil. The amount of hydrogen ions determines how acid
(sour) or alkaline (sweet) a soil is. (See Table 10–2.)

TABLE 10–2

pH Values of Common Items

Lemon juice	2.3	
Orange juice	3.8	acid (sour)
Sour milk	4.8	
Fresh milk	6.6	
Water (free of minerals)	7.0	neutral
Blood	7.3	
Sea water	7.9	alkaline (sweet)
Soap solutions	9.5	

342. Does the soil pH indicate when lime should be added to the lawn?

Yes, the object of adding lime is to raise the soil pH into the
favorable range for grass growth. This means that any time you
have a soil pH below 6.0 you should consider liming your lawn.
Never add lime to your lawn if the pH is above 6.0 (See Tables
10–3, 10–4, and 10–5.)

343. When I'm leveling the soil around my house prior to seeding, should the soil be even, lower, or higher than the surface of the sidewalks?

It is best to leave the soil one inch lower than the sidewalk
levels. This allows the lawn to look even with the sidewalks after
the lawn has been mowed.

344. How important is it to have the lawn sloping away from the foundation of my house?

There should always be enough slope away from the house so
that water will not stand next to the foundation and seep into the

TABLE 10–3
Liming Chart

Soil pH	Pounds of lime per 1,000 sq. ft. of lawn	
	Light soil (sandy)	*Heavy soil (clayey)*
5.0	70	150
5.5	45	120
6.0	25	60
6.5	none	none

TABLE 10–4

The soil pH ranges from 1 to 14. Most lawn grasses do best when the pH is in the range of 6.0 to 7.6

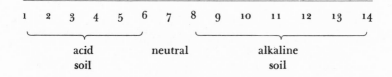

| 1 | 2 | 3 | 4 | 5 | 6 | 7 | 8 | 9 | 10 | 11 | 12 | 13 | 14 |

acid soil   neutral   alkaline soil

TABLE 10–5
List of Turfgrasses and the pH Ranges in Which They Will Grow

Grasses	pH Range
Bentgrass	5.5 to 7.5
Bermudagrass	5.0 to 7.0
Buffalograss	6.1 to 8.6
Carpetgrass	4.8 to 7.0
Centipedegrass	4.0 to 6.0
Chewing Fescue	5.4 to 7.6
Kentucky Bluegrass	6.0 to 7.6
Red Fescue	5.4 to 7.6
Ryegrass	5.4 to 8.0
St. Augustinegrass	6.0 to 8.0
Zoysia	4.6 to 7.6

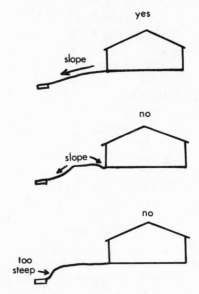

Figure 10–4. A slope greater than 10% or less than 1% around your home can cause drainage problems.

basement. A 1 percent slope is the minimum you should consider, while a 10 percent slope should be the maximum. A steep slope is hard to keep grass on and makes mowing difficult. (See fig. 10–4.)

345. Should I save the topsoil from the lot where my new home is to be built?

Yes. It should be written in the contract that the topsoil is to be pushed to the side during construction and spread evenly over the lawn area after construction is finished. It is important that the soil is not extremely wet when it is being moved. Be sure no foreign objects (for example, boards, rocks, concrete) are buried under the topsoil.

346. Is there any way to get rid of moles other than using bait or traps?

The best way to keep moles out of your lawn is to first get rid of their food supply. Once this is done they will stay out of your lawn. Grubs are the main source of food for moles, so use an insecticide such as diazinon to get rid of them.

347. My three-gallon, hand-pressurized sprayer is always causing me problems. What do I do wrong?

The two most prominent reasons for sprayer failure are clogged nozzles and rusty, corroded parts. Simple, preventive maintenance will solve both problems. Corrosion of your sprayer is easily avoided by not using it as a storage tank for leftover solution. Many chemicals clump up after sitting for any length of time and clog the hoses and nozzles. Also, the salts in the solution will corrode the metal and will cause the moving parts to become stuck. Always empty your sprayer when you are through and rinse it out thoroughly. This increases the life of your sprayer and insures you it will work the next time it is needed.

348. What can cause the nozzle of a sprayer to become clogged if I don't store leftover chemicals in it?

Clogging of nozzles can be caused by the accidental introduction of foreign material (grass clippings, dust, sand, leaves, soil, twigs) into the sprayer while you are filling it or while the lid is off. If the nozzle becomes clogged, you can use a fine wire to clean the openings.

349. What is the best way to clean my sprayer when I'm through using it?

After you have completed spraying your lawn, you should wash out the sprayer with either ammonia (¼ cup) or a small amount of household detergent mixed with water. Use this solution and rinse the sprayer thoroughly. Don't forget to run some of the solution through the hose and nozzle. And then take an absorbent cloth and wipe the sprayer dry.

350. What are some tips on good maintenance practices for my drop-spreader?

The most important maintenance practice is to always empty the excess material back into the bag and then wash the spreader with water from the garden hose. Use a cloth to dry the spreader before putting it away. Excess material will absorb moisture from the air and cause the spreader to gum up, clogging the delivery holes. Oil the moving parts at the beginning of the growing season and when you put the spreader away at the end of the year. Wipe off the excess oil. Use a wire brush to remove any rust you see. Cover the exposed metal with a resistant paint to prevent future problems.

351. What should be done with any chemicals left over after treating my lawn for pests?

Read the label on the container; it should tell you how long a shelf-life the chemical has after being opened. Mark the container when you first open it so you know when it is time to dispose of it. The best solution is to buy the right size of container so that the contents can be used in the prescribed time. If you do need to get rid of excess material, it is best to bury it in a tight container in the ground, where it will not contaminate any water in the area and where children or animals cannot find it and dig it up.

352. Is there any harm in walking across grass when there is frost on the ground?

Yes. Walking across a frost-covered lawn will damage the grass every place you step. Because the plant cells are frozen, the cells are crushed when you step on them. In a matter of hours, as the temperature rises, the crushed grass will stand out as black footprints on an otherwise green lawn.

353. Does it hurt the grass to put off raking leaves until all have fallen from the trees?

If the leaves completely cover the grass, there is a possibility that the grass will be smothered. This is especially true if the leaves become wet and the added weight presses the grass flat on the ground. If enough light doesn't penetrate the leaves, the grass could suffer and even die.

354. Do the leaves have enough nutrients in them to do the grass any good?

The fallen leaves have very little nutritional value in them so they should not be left on the grass to act as a fertilizer. The leaves can, however, be raked up and added to your compost pile.

355. What are some of the hazards from burning leaves?

The careless burning of leaves has caused the death of many trees, shrubs, and lawns. Never burn leaves near desirable plants, since they are more susceptible to heat damage than people. Burning leaves under a tree will usually result in the killing of the limbs overhanging the fire. The burning of leaves is also considered a form of air pollution, and some states have passed laws against this practice.

356. Will the salt I use on my sidewalks during the winter do any damage to my grass?

In small amounts the salt will not damage the grass. If a large concentration is allowed to build up along the edges of the side-walks, the grass could be damaged. Usually spring rains and the melting snow will wash the salt away.

357. How can I get grass established quickly in the bare spots in my lawn?

If you do not want to use seed, cut pieces of sod from the edge of your lawn and put them on the bare spots. Be sure to loosen the soil so the roots from the sod will knit quickly. Water the new sod frequently during the first two weeks.

358. Is it a good idea to use fertilizers that have herbicides and insecticides mixed in with them?

The combination of fertilizers and pesticides will save the homeowner the extra work of applying each one separately. The chemicals mixed in with the fertilizer may or may not be harmful to your flowers, trees, and shrubs. Read the label; it will tell you which flowers and shrubs the chemical will not damage. Also, check for a list of the pests the chemical will control.

359. What can be done to save a tree when putting three feet of soil over the existing lawn?

Build a stone wall around the base of the tree. It should be approximately three feet from the tree to the edge of the wall. Tile drains should be put down in the ground at the drip line of the tree so that water and air can get to the roots. A shallow layer of coarse gravel or rocks placed on top of the old grade will also help to trap air for the roots. (See fig. 10–5.)

360. When I'm planning the landscape around my house, do the trees I select have any bearing, other than shade, on the quality of lawn I will be able to grow?

Usually, shading is the biggest problem trees cause to the lawn. However, there are other factors you should be aware of.

Tree roots are great at robbing the moisture and plant nutrients from the soil. This is especially true near the surface of the soil, where the grass roots are growing. Tree roots are also famous for surfacing and causing a rough bumpy lawn. To overcome these two inconveniences, try planting the trees as far away from the main lawn area as possible.

Consider the size of the leaf when selecting your trees. Large leaves, as on maples and oaks, will smother the grass if not removed in the fall. Fine leaves, as on the willow, Russian olive, and locust, cause fewer problems and do not always require fall raking.

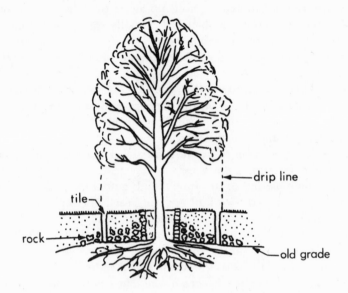

tile

drip line

rock

old grade

Figure 10–5. If you have to fill around trees, provide extra drainage and air to their roots. *Courtesy of Indiana Cooperative Extension Service, Purdue University, West Lafayette, Indiana.*

Consider also whether the tree is male or female. Plant a male tree whenever possible, and you won't be bothered all the time with seedling trees coming up in your lawn and garden.

361. I would like to include shade trees in my landscaping, but I would also like to have a nice lawn. Can I have both?

It will be difficult to grow grass under any of the larger shade trees when they reach maturity. This is especially true if two or three are planted close enough for their branches to touch each other. Some examples of large shade trees would be the Norway maple, silver maple, red oak, elm, and ash.

To provide shade in your yard, select one of the smaller-growing trees—one that will blend with your landscaping rather than overpower it in years to come. I like the flowering crabtree, hawthorn, horse chestnut, or apple and peach trees for this purpose. The limbs should be pruned high enough above the ground so you can walk under the tree. A single tree of this group will allow the grass to grow under it readily.

362. I have a lawn that is very thin due to three beautiful maple trees on my lot. What can I do to get a better stand of grass?

You must decide which is the more important to you, the shade or the lawn. It will always be difficult to grow grass under those three maples. If you want the shade, then improve the soil drainage, fertilize frequently, overseed often, mow the grass high rather than low, and use shade-tolerant grasses. Consider removing one of the maples; this would let in enough light to have a nice lawn, and you will hardly miss the tree once it's gone.

363. Is there any set plan for locating new trees around my lawn so the grass won't be shaded too much?

Yes. Locate a tree or two on the north side of your yard. The shade from these trees will always be cast off to the side, allowing sunshine to reach the grass below. You should take into consideration your neighbor's grass and discuss your plans with them. The shade from your trees could easily make it difficult for the grass to grow in their lawn. If you suspect a problem is going to develop, it is best to consider landscaping the north side of your lot with shrubs and dwarf trees.

Of more importance to your lawn's well-being is the location of trees on the south side of your lot. If you plant trees on the south side, then be sure to leave sufficient space between them for the sunlight to reach the grass for at least four to eight hours a day. Morning sun is best for the grass.

Be sure to locate at least one shade tree on the southwest side of your house. This tree will provide shade for the house, and this will help to reduce the inside temperature of your home.

364. You have said that a nice lawn increases the value of a home. Is this also true for shade trees?

Trees definitely make a home worth more. Whether they are for your own enjoyment or for the eventual sale of your house, they add a great deal to the value of your land.

Shade trees established around a home will generally increase the overall value of your property by $3,000 to $6,000. The exact amount varies according to the type of trees, number present, and their location.

365. How can I plan my flower and shrub beds so they do not cause me problems getting a mower around them?

When first laying out the various garden beds on your lot, consider how sharp a turn you can make with a lawn mower. Stretch a rope over the area where the edge of the bed will extend. Walk your mower along the rope to determine the ease of mowing along the proposed bed.

You want free-flowing, long-sweeping curves. These same gentle lines will give you an attractive edge, enhancing your flowerbeds and shrub beds and the entire lawn. Do not have any plants too close to the edge of the bed. Overhanging plants will get cut off by the mower, destroying them and the appearance of your lawn.

366. I'm getting very tired of trimming grass along the house and flowerbeds. Is there any way to reduce this unpleasant task?

There is a simple solution to your problem. It will take some work on your part but when finished will be well worth the effort.

A mowing strip around the edges of your lawn of either brick, concrete blocks, or even a four-inch strip of concrete will give you a permanent edge over which you can run one wheel of your mower and clip all the grass. This will eliminate that hand-clipping job, which is so bothersome and tiring.

367. Across the front of my yard is a steep, six-foot bank that is difficult to mow. The neighborhood children use it for their "king of the mountain" games, wearing bare spots in the lawn. What can be done to this problem area?

Your problem could be solved very easily by constructing a low wall. Several different types of material may be selected for the job: concrete block, brick, large river rock, flat stone, railroad ties, cement pipe, telephone poles, or a poured concrete wall. Select a material that will enhance your home and the rest of your landscape.

The height of the wall will be determined by many factors. Cost of material, amount and height of slope, and your other plans for the area. You also want the wall to be high enough so the new grade will be easy to mow.

368. What is the best way to manage a lawn area that has constant foot traffic?

Why not consider a sidewalk or rock walkway? Trying to grow grass in a natural pathway is very difficult. In fact, it is often impossible, and the worn-out grass detracts from the appearance of the rest of the yard.

A gently curving sidewalk will look much more attractive than a straight-edged one. The use of flat rocks or preconstructed patio pieces inlaid makes an attractive walk. These blend in well with the grass and give the walk a more natural look. Your choice depends on personal preference and the location of the walkway.

Remember to keep the top of the walkway level with the existing soil. This allows the mower to do a total job and eliminates bothersome hand-clipping.

369. After a new home is built, which should you do first, put in the lawn or landscape the lot?

The lawn should be graded, fertilized, and seeded or sodded prior to planting shrubs and trees. Because grass takes longer to establish itself, the lawn should be done as soon as possible.

Before you start the lawn, first complete all sidewalks and drives. Trucks and other heavy equipment will really tear up the soil around the area where they are being used. If you have worked hard getting the lawn started, you will be very upset at the damage done to the area. By waiting until this job is over, you will have to grade the soil up to the hard-surfaced areas only once, thus reducing the amount of work it takes to get your new lawn started.

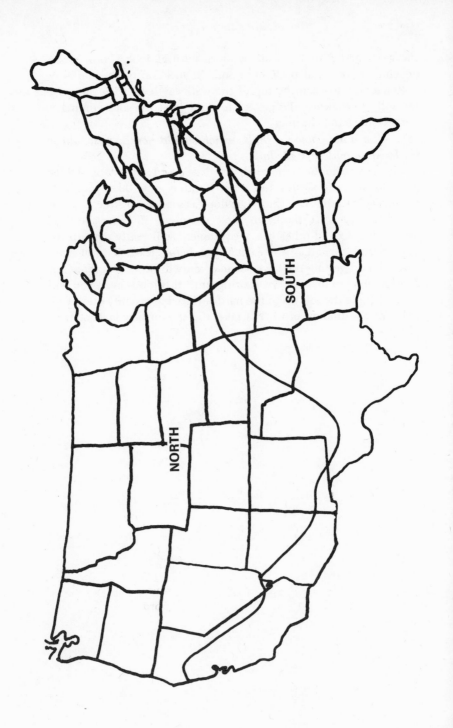

11

Your Year-Round Guide for Lawn Care

Up to this point you have been learning, piece by piece, how to grow grass and manipulate it into the best darn lawn in the neighborhood! You've read about grass varieties, fertilizer ratios and grades, seeding rates, correct watering practices, how to choose a lawn mower, perennial and annual weeds, disease and insect control, and something called soil texture. Now it is time to wrap it all up into one neat, easy-to-understand package—something you can glance at, month by month, and use as a guide in your lawn-care activities.

Remember what you learned in Chapter 2 about the United States being divided into different growing regions for grasses. These regions can be classified as North and South. Check the map to determine which lawn-care guide you should follow.

Keep in mind the importance of staying in tune with Mother Nature's schedule. Time your lawn-care endeavors so they are harmonious with hers. This is the key to being successful with your lawn or any other gardening project you undertake. The purpose of this chapter is to take all the pieces of the lawn-care puzzle and put them together for you, thus handing you the "key" to a successful lawn-care program.

The techniques discussed in the month-by-month guide are not explained in full, but enough information is presented so you can easily understand what should be accomplished. Check the previous chapters to refresh your memory on any of the lawn-care procedures you may have forgotten or want to be sure you understand. A few minutes spent rereading a question or two and the answers may save you a costly mistake later.

JANUARY

North

With temperatures outside ranging from minus 30 to plus 30 degrees, the last thing anyone wants to consider is working on the lawn. Occasionally, the vision of arriving spring, green grass, and flowers flashes across the mind and brings back pleasant memories. However, it is still two to three months before any earnest outdoor work can begin. Sit back in your easy chair, relax, and read a good book.

South

Unless you live in southern Florida, this month should not see you doing a lot of lawn work. Although the weather is frequently warm enough for you to go outside in short sleeves, the cooler days and evenings have caused the grass to stop growing. But Floridians may find that their lawns have grown a little and an occasional mowing may be necessary.

FEBRUARY

North

The days are still short, snow covers the ground, and winter weather has a firm grip on the landscape. Now is the time to start reading the magazines and checking the advertisements for lawn and garden catalogues. In another month the grass will be growing at the southern edges of this region.

South

Warm weather has reached up into northern Florida, and the days are slowly getting longer. If the Bermudagrass or St. Augustinegrass has continued to grow through January and this month, then it will need ½ pound of nitrogen per 1,000 square feet to keep it healthy and to give it a boost into the spring months.

Control of those pesty annual weeds should begin near the end of February if you live in Florida or along the Gulf of Mexico or in southern California. Crabgrass and annual bluegrass are two of the culprits you are out to get.

If the grass has started to grow, watering your lawn may become necessary if it hasn't rained.

MARCH

North

At last a few warm days in which the homeowner can venture outside and begin the spring yardwork. Your lawn-care activities should be limited to two items at this time. This is when you should spend some time cleaning up the debris that accumulated over the winter. While picking up, survey your lawn for any signs that indicate it may need special attention this coming spring. Next month you should launch a full-scale lawn-care program, based on what you saw and using this guide's recommendations.

The other possible lawn-care activity to initiate now is that of overseeding any bare or thinned-out spots in the lawn. Seed a good lawn grass at 1 to 2 pounds of seed per 1,000 square feet. (Check Chapter 4 for the specific number of seeds to sow per square inch on small bare spots.) This seed will lie on top of the ground and germinate as the weather warms up.

South

A few items need to be considered, all of which are important if you want a nice lawn. First, let's pick up a little unfinished business left over from last month. Along the Atlantic seacoast, and in southern Georgia, Alabama, and Mississippi, the control of crabgrass, annual bluegrass, and other annual grasses should be nearly completed. If you live in Louisiana or southern Texas, you should have put crabgrass preventive chemicals on your lawn by this time. Check at the local garden center for the best products to use in your area.

Three of the more prominent Southern grasses (Bermudagrass, St. Augustinegrass, and zoysia) should be fertilized. Apply a good turf fertilizer at a rate of 2 pounds of nitrogen per 1,000 square feet. This feeding will supply the grass plants with the food needed throughout the spring months, causing a nice, dark-green lawn. This is one step in your lawn-care program that should never be skipped.

As the grass growth begins to respond to the warmer days, the need to mow and water regularly becomes essential. Don't let the grass grow to a height beyond that at which you plan to mow. For example, if you are going to mow the grass at a one-inch height, then don't let it get longer than two inches between mowings. Removing too much of the leaf blade at a single mowing can weaken the grass and open the door to disease and insects.

APRIL

North

The weather will play a major role as to when you start your lawn-care program in earnest. Be ready to mow the grass for the first time as soon as it starts to grow. This will remove all the dead grass tops and will allow the lawn to green-up more quickly in the spring.

All the Northern grasses need to be fertilized this month so they will begin actively growing early in the spring. Apply 2 pounds of nitrogen per 1,000 square feet for the best results.

If crabgrass, foxtail, or barnyardgrass were a problem in your lawn last year, consider doing something about it now. Check the crabgrass germination map on page 88 to determine the best time to begin taking preventive measures to assure that crabgrass will not be a problem again. There are several preemergent weed killers on the market, and all do a good job, provided you put them on before the weed seeds germinate. Use 2,4-D, available in liquid or granular form, to rid your lawn of those pesty broadleaf weeds —dandelions, clover, plantain, and shepherd's-purse. Don't expect the weeds to disappear overnight after spraying; it may be 7 to 10 days before they curl up and die.

A couple of diseases, helminthosporium leafspot and snow mold, may cause problems early in the spring. If there had been a heavy snow on the ground, followed by a wet spring, be watchful for disease problems.

Be on the lookout for insects trying to eat up your grass. Grubs, ants, wireworms, armyworms, cutworms, chiggers, and crickets are a few of the little creatures to be on the alert for.

South

All Bahiagrass, carpetgrass, centipedegrass, and Bermudagrass lawns need to be fertilized with 1 pound of nitrogen per 1,000 square feet. This should be the second feeding for the Bermudagrass lawns. Use a complete fertilizer (nitrogen, phosphorus, and potassium) for the best results.

Should you have any bare spots in your lawn, obtain sprigs or plugs from the edge of your lawn and use them for fill-in material. This would be an excellent time to go to the garden center and buy some sprigs or plugs of the newer grass varieties available and begin to upgrade your lawn.

Aerification and thatch removal are two manicuring techniques that really improve your lawn. Power machines are available at most rental stores for a modest fee. Get a couple of your neighbors to join you and split the cost.

Grass that stays yellow and doesn't green-up may have insects at the root of the problem. Get down on your hands and knees and play Sherlock Holmes. If your investigation doesn't turn up any signs of insects, perhaps iron deficiency, poor water drainage, a need for lime, diseases, or pet damage could be causing the trouble.

Crabgrass control chemicals should be applied to lawns by the end of April in states located at the northern limits of the Southern grass region.

MAY

North

Your lawn should be one of the nicest on the block by now, especially after fertilizing last month and overseeding early in the year. Sharpen your lawn-mower blade, and don't let the grass go too long between mowings. One of the secrets of having a beautiful lawn is to mow frequently, giving the grass that manicured look.

If a few "yellow-heads," otherwise known as dandelions, are still present, give them another dose of 2,4-D. Be careful not to get any of this chemical on the flowers or shrubs because it will kill them too. It is still not too late to control crabgrass in the Northern states. By the end of May, however, don't use preemergent weed-killer to kill crabgrass in states in the lower half of the Northern grass region. Unless it is a really serious problem, once the crabgrass seed has germinated, there is nothing you can do about it until the following spring. There are some chemicals at the garden center to spray on young crabgrass plants to kill them. Read the instructions carefully if you decide to use them.

South

Now is the perfect time to start a new lawn. The days are sunny and warm, with the hot summer days not too far off. Use seeds, sprigs, plugs, or sod—whatever fits your needs. The quickest lawn can be obtained by sodding, but it is also the most expensive. Sprigging is usually the most common in the South. Sprigging a lawn takes two to three months for the grass to fill in and be ready for children to play on. Bermudagrass and St. Augustinegrass are frequently sprigged into lawn areas, while zoysia is usually started from plugs. By the way, it is not too late to work on any bare or thin spots in an old lawn. The Southern grasses really flourish in the hot, humid weather, so get them started now and they will be ready to thrive under the blazing summer sun.

Broadleaf weeds, such as plantain, sheep sorrel, dandelions, yellow oxalis, chickweed, and clover can become a nuisance in a lawn if left alone. Buy some 2,4-D at any garden center. Sometimes it takes two applications, 8 to 10 days apart, to kill some of the more stubborn weeds. Be careful not to spray flowers and shrubs, or they will die also.

Mow as frequently as the grass needs it, never removing more than one half of the grass blade at a cutting. Check the mower blade and determine if it needs to be sharpened. A dull mower blade damages the grass and is hard on the lawn mower.

JUNE

North

Growth of the cool-weather grasses will start slowing down if the weather is hot and dry. To counteract this you need to fertilize and water. Spreading 1 pound of nitrogen per 1,000 square feet will give the grass an extra energy boost and, with frequent watering, you will be supplying the plants with the essential ingredients through the summer months.

Inspect the lawn for anything looking like a disease problem. Hot, humid days encourage the disease organisms to attack the grass. Pythium, dollar spot, and fusarium blight are just three of the rascals you may have to battle. If a problem exists, make a quick trip to the garden center for a fungicide spray.

South

It is still possible to start a new lawn if you didn't get it done last month. The sooner you can get the grass growing, the better your chances are for full coverage by fall. The need to water frequently, not letting the new grass dry out, is critical. It would be a shame to spend money on getting a lawn started and then assume Mother Nature will do the remainder of your work for you. Those bare spots in your lawn can still be sprigged or plugged in June also.

The intrusion of insects should be expected at this time. Chinch bugs, grubs, sod webworms, mole crickets, and armyworms are a few of the regular pests. Try to identify the insect before you start spraying chemicals to kill them; this will allow you to select the proper insecticide for the job. Remember, all insects are not harmful to the grass and therefore shouldn't be sprayed just because of their presence, unless they become a nuisance.

Bermudagrass, zoysia, and carpetgrass lawns could all use another fertilizer application to keep them actively growing during this prime grass-growing time of the year. The addition of the extra one to two pounds of nitrogen on a Bermudagrass lawn is essential now and should not be skipped. The zoysia and carpetgrass can wait another month before being fertilized, provided they were fed in the spring.

JULY

North and South

You are now half way through the growing season, and it's all downhill from here on in. All grasses would benefit if you raised the height of your mower blade. In the North a full inch would be adequate, while down South a half inch will do the job. The increased length of the grass blade will allow extra food to be manufactured. The longer grass blade will also shade the ground to help lower the temperature around the grass and reduce water evaporation.

Remember, an occasional watering may be necessary, depending on the weather. This is a good time to sit back in your lawn chair and enjoy the fruits of your labor.

AUGUST

North

After a leisurely Fourth of July, you are now looking forward to Labor Day, your next holiday. Don't forget about your lawn during this time.

The cool-season grasses (bluegrass, ryegrass, bentgrass, fescue, and zoysia) prefer the fall rains and cool weather for growing. A new lawn should be started any time now. Try to have your seed in the ground and watered at least once by the end of this month. The longer the grass has to grow before the first snow arrives, the better the lawn will be the following spring.

Are there small, tan-colored moths flittering across your lawn during the evening? If yes, then sod webworms are your problem. They are laying thousands of eggs that will very slowly hatch into hungry caterpillars. Two other insects, grubs and armyworms, may become a nuisance, too. All three pests are easy to control with one or two applications of an insecticide.

Many Northern lawns are infested with a weedy grass called *Poa annua* or annual bluegrass. It can be easily identified at this time of the year by the prolific seedheads it produces, even when mowed short, and by its light-green color. Ridding it from your lawn is not an easy task, and, in fact, most homeowners don't even worry about it. It is unattractive, and if you want to keep your lawn free of this blemish, the necessary chemicals need to be applied. It might require another dose of preemergent herbicide in April to finish the job. *Poa annua* is a tenacious plant, easy to get into your lawn and very difficult to get rid of.

South

During the long, hot days, the grass will suffer if there isn't any moisture in the soil. A good watering once a week will keep the grass growing and allow it to retain the deep-green color expected from a lawn. The best time for watering is in the morning. This allows the grass to dry off in the afternoon sun and stops most disease problems before they have a chance to get started. Watering the lawn once a week means you will continue the mowing program all through the summer.

Diseases may attack your grass if the weather conditions are favorable. They are not a major problem for the homeowner, but be aware and keep a watchful eye. If a disease does show up, spray a broad-spectrum fungicide on your lawn.

Poa annua (annual bluegrass) is about ready to start seeding again. If you want to keep it out of your lawn, get that preemergent chemical down. It forms a barrier in the soil, killing the seeds of this pest as they sprout.

SEPTEMBER

North

With winter not too far away, the grass needs to be prepared for the long, cold months ahead. One essential step for this preparation is the application of a balanced fertilizer, one containing nitrogen, phophorus, and potassium. Apply about 2 pounds of nitrogen per 1,000 square feet of lawn area. This feeding keeps the grass growing healthily right up to the cool weather, with some of the plant food stored and left over for use by the plant next spring. This gives the grass a little boost until you get the spring fertilizer application on the lawn.

Overseeding into a poor lawn may be done only if you live along the southern boundaries of the North grass region. The grass seed must have four to six weeks of good weather left after germination if it is to survive the winter weather.

Broadleaf weeds still present in your lawn should be treated with 2,4-D, just as the flowers are starting to seed. Do not spray weeds in a new lawn just getting started. Young grass seedlings are very susceptible to 2,4-D. Two or three mowings will eliminate most of the weeds; spray the rest next spring.

Thatch, a layer of dead and decaying plant matter located at the soil surface, should be thinned out if it is more than a half inch thick. Power rakes and verticut machines are available from most rental businesses. Removing this excessive organic layer will give the grass more vigor, allow the water from rainfall and irrigation to soak into the soil, lower the chances of having a disease or insect problem, and let more air into the soil, where the plant roots really need it.

South

You are coming into the homestretch and there aren't too many things left to do for the grass before the cooler days arrive. An application of a balanced fertilizer is in order at this time. Pick a good turf fertilizer at the store and give the grass about 2 pounds of nitrogen per 1,000 square feet. If you have a Bermudagrass lawn, cut the application rate in half and put the other half on next month. This will help even out the growth of the Bermuda-grass over the next couple of months. Don't skip fertilizing your lawn in the fall; it is an important ingredient to having a beautiful lawn.

If there is a layer of dead, decaying plant material underneath the green grass, rent a power rake or verticut machine to remove the layer. This thatch restricts water and air movement into the rootzone, and this weakens the grass, making it more susceptible to damage from diseases and insects.

Another procedure to consider, which will be very beneficial to the lawn in most instances, is aerification. Again you can rent an aerifier and do the lawn in a day without any trouble. When the soil is compacted and hard as a rock, aerification is an excellent technique to loosen the soil and make room for the roots to grow.

OCTOBER

North

There isn't much left to do to the lawn now. Winter is just a few weeks away, and there aren't many warm days left. The need for watering and mowing has tapered off and just about been forgotten. Don't put the mower away until the lawn has been cut one last time after the grass has stopped growing. Long, uncut grass tends to mat and smother the grass, leaving brown spots next spring.

Tree leaves should be raked up and hauled away. Leaves left on the grass, even a single leaf, will smother the grass and leave an unsightly lawn for you next spring.

South

A brown, dormant grass does not add much to the beauty of the landscape around the home. Green-up the brown lawn by over-seeding a winter grass into it. Bluegrass and ryegrass may be used for this job. Topdress the seed, and you will get a higher percentage of germination.

Continue sprinkling the lawn whenever the rainfalls are inadequate. This helps to keep the grass nice and green, right up to the cold weather of winter. So long as the weather is warm and sufficient water is available, the grass will continue to grow, and so an occasional mowing will be necessary.

Never will there be a better time to rid your lawn of those bothersome broadleaf weeds. Dandelions, clover, and yellow oxalis all will succumb to an application of 2,4-D at this time. Don't miss this excellent opportunity to get the upper hand on weeds in your lawn.

NOVEMBER

North

Liming a lawn is sometimes necessary if a soil test has shown the soil pH to be lower than 6.0. Spread an agricultural grade of lime on the lawn, being careful not to skip any part of the yard. The winter snows and rains will wash the lime into the ground, where it will be ready to go to work for you next spring. Another application may be needed again next year, but only a soil test can determine this.

Preventive maintenance on your lawn equipment will save you from having to buy new equipment every year. Spend one Saturday winterizing your lawn mower, assuring it will be ready for use next spring. Tune the engine of the mower, check and clean both the electric and fuel systems, grease all moving parts, change oil, and sharpen and balance the mower blade.

South

The winter grasses sown last month should have sprouted and started to green-up your lawn by now. Applying a fertilizer will give these grasses the necessary plant food to carry them over through the winter months. Two pounds of nitrogen per 1,000 square feet is all that is needed.

If you didn't want to be bothered with mowing and fertilizing your lawn this winter, but wish it would stay green, you have one option left. There are five or six different kinds of green dyes available for spraying the lawn; check the local garden center to see what they suggest. These "turf colorants" do a good job of changing a dull-brown, lifeless grass into a lively, sparkling lawn you can enjoy all winter.

DECEMBER

North and South

This is the month for rest and relaxation. Reflect back on the previous year's work and discover which goals you reached and what new ones need to be formulated for next year. Was your lawn a success? Did you spend too much money on it? Or too little? Were your lawn-care practices in tune with Mother Nature's schedule? Answering these types of questions will give you an idea of how well your lawn did in the past year and what its chances of success are in the coming year.

Maintaining a nice lawn is not a difficult job. Once you have an understanding of what the grass's requirements are and know the best time to accomplish each lawn-care task, you will become the lawn-care expert in your neighborhood.

12

Ground Covers: A Natural Carpet for Your Enjoyment

Have you ever considered planting part of your lawn with a ground cover rather than seeding it all in grass? If you haven't thought of it before now, consider it for a few minutes. With the addition of a ground cover, you can add interest to the landscape around your home or improve problem areas where the grass never seems to do well.

A good example of this occurred in my own yard. I had in the center of my yard a big maple tree that kept the grass beneath it thin and struggling to stay alive. To solve the problem I built a 20-foot-diameter rock wall, 6 inches high, around the tree and planted *Euonymus fortunei* colorata (purple wintercreeper). In one year's time I turned the base of that maple tree into one of the prettiest spots in my yard. The overall affect of the combination of the maple tree, grass, and ground cover created a more balanced landscaping, each element complementing the other.

There are other instances where a ground cover may be used in place of grass. Shady spots are the first place you should think of. Unless the sun shines on the lawn about half a day, grass plants will not do well, even with watering and fertilizing. There are several ground covers that do well in shade and can be used in place of grass very conveniently. Carpet bugle, ivy, ferns, lily-of-the-valley, periwinkle, and wintercreeper all tolerate shade conditions.

Steep banks are difficult to mow and often become deeply rutted and unsightly. Sometimes a strip, too narrow to mow, causes you a maintenance headache, and you wish for a simple solution each time you look at it. In both these cases ground covers can be used to improve the appearance of your lawn.

A more specialized use for ground covers is obvious whenever you visit a beach area and see the homes built among the rocks and sand overlooking the water. Dry, sandy conditions and a salt problem make it next to impossible to grow grass, yet there are several plants that have adapted to this environment. Bearberry, rugosa roses, shore juniper, and beach wormwood can help stabilize the sand and soil, while adding a touch of beauty to an area that may otherwise be barren.

Several other circumstances may give you an opportunity to consider using a ground cover. Tree roots surfacing in the lawn from that large shade tree create a problem when you're mowing, cause an unsightly lawn, and can even be a hazard when you're taking your late evening stroll around the yard. Chopping them out with an axe is tiring and doesn't completely solve the problem. A better solution is to use low-growing plants to cover the area.

Often a rock wall or an outcropping of rocks and boulders presents a nice opportunity for using small plants interspersed in the crevices. The two different textures (rocks and plants) make an attractive arrangement in any location. Careful selection of native materials usually works best under these circumstances.

Another advantage of ground covers is that newly planted shrub beds are enhanced by low-growing plants, and weeds will be discouraged. At the same time, you have provided added interest around the base of your shrubs.

Do you have a flowerbed full of tulips, crocus, narcissus, lilies, or any of the other numerous bulbous plants? If so, then ground covers are made to order for you. Plants that grow from bulbs prefer to have their roots shaded from the direct sunlight. A ground cover readily provides cooling shade and also offers contrasting plant foliage for a touch of elegance in your flowerbeds. Weeds will be less of a problem once the ground cover becomes established in your perennial flowerbeds.

Finally, if you just don't want to spend all your time mowing, watering, fertilizing, and weeding a lawn, a ground cover will give you an almost maintenance-free landscape. You'll still have to take care of the plants, but their needs are easy to meet.

Often a wide-open lawn, bordered by a few trees and flowerbeds, will look nice but may lack that little extra something to really set it apart from the neighbor's. Ground covers can easily do the job for you. They come in a wide variety of shapes and colors that will allow you to choose a texture and form that will really make your yard stand out. In the following pages I discuss ground covers and how to plant and maintain them. I also list many of the plants according to special categories, such as shade-tolerant plants and those for use along the seaside. For your convenience there is also a Ground-Cover Hardiness Map showing where various plants will and will not grow.

A drive around the residential areas of your city will give you some ideas of how other homeowners have used ground covers to accentuate their landscape. With a little imagination, it shouldn't take you long to find a way to incorporate some ground-cover plants around your home, whether for the aesthetic values or for solving a maintenance headache.

13

Planting Your Ground Cover

The most common reason for failure of a new ground-cover planting is the lack of proper soil preparation. Just as you work the soil prior to seeding your lawn or before planting flowers, so must you do the same for a ground-cover plant. Its roots require the same type of bed as any other plant.

Work the soil until it is loosened 6 inches to 10 inches deep. Avoid tilling the soil if it is too wet. The soil should easily crumble in your hands when it is ready for you to begin.

IMPROVING THE SOIL

A soil with a lot of clay in it (sticky when moist) or one that is mostly sand can be improved with the incorporation of organic materials. There are several kinds available. Your choice will depend upon what is locally available to you at a reasonable price. In the larger areas you may use peat moss or well-rotted manure. For a small spot, you may wish to use some organic material from your compost pile. Leafmold or sawdust are two other possibilities to consider.

Whatever you select, spread it about two or three inches thick over the worked soil. Mix the organic material, by tilling, uniformly into the soil as deep as you can.

Organic material does several things for you. It binds the soil into small aggregates, leaving air pockets in the soil where plant roots can proliferate. The water-holding capacity of a soil is markedly improved by the addition of these dead plant materials. Bacteria and other important soil organisms use the organic material as a source of food and then release nutrients from it for the plant. Finally the organic material makes the soil easier for you to work with and increases the overall ability of the soil to accept and support plant life.

One other area needs to be discussed before looking at some of the other requirements of ground-cover plants. After telling you about the need to loosen the soil before planting, I must include one case where the rule must be bent to fit a particular circumstance.

PREPARATION OF A SLOPE

A soil bank, regardless of how steep, would tend to erode and wash away if you loosen the entire bank. When this happens you really have a problem. Yet, if you are to successfully grow a ground cover on the bank, what are you to do?

Special nettings that can be stretched over bare soil are now available. They protect the soil while the plants are getting established and sending down roots to bind the soil together. If you use this technique, be sure the netting will decompose if left on the bank. A plastic or rubberized netting should not be used.

Another approach is to dig up small areas where the plants are to be set. This gives them a chance to become entrenched in a good soil bed before trying to gain a foothold in the less hospitable soil around it. This will work very well, but you must be careful when watering or you may wash much of the soil down the nearest storm sewer openings.

KNOW THE SOIL pH

One property of the soil you need to be aware of before selecting any type of a ground cover is the soil reaction or pH of the soil. This topic was covered in Chapter 10 and you may wish to refer to it.

It is possible to choose the wrong plant for a particular soil. If your soil is alkaline (sweet), then it would be a mistake to plant wintergreen, pachistima, or bloodroot plants that flourish in acid soils and do poorly in alkaline ones.

Kits are available, at most garden centers, for use in testing the soil pH. The amount of money you will pay for one of these kits is nominal when you consider the investment of your time and money to set out a ground-cover bed.

Lime should not be added to the soil unless the pH of a soil test indicates it is needed. Don't let your neighbors talk you into adding lime unless you know the soil needs it!

ENRICHING THE SOIL IS IMPORTANT

While you have the soil loose, and just prior to mixing in the organic material, spread some fertilizer on the soil. Use a complete plant food that contains nitrogen, phosphorus, and potassium. Select one with the numbers 10–10–10, 12–12–12, or 16–8–8 on the bag. Apply 1½ to 2 pounds of fertilizer per 100 square feet of soil area.

When you mix the organic material into the soil, you will also be distributing the fertilizer throughout the soil where the plant roots can readily absorb it. This is essential if your plants are to become rapidly established and spread quickly over the surface of the soil.

It is a fact that any time you add two or three inches of organic material to a soil, you will also need to mix in a nitrogen fertilizer. Nitrogen is used by the soil bacteria when they break down the organic material. This causes a temporary shortage of nitrogen, which you will need to replenish by adding a fertilizer along with the organic material.

CONTROL THOSE PESTY WEEDS

The final step in soil preparation is an important one. Complete weed eradication is a must if your ground cover is to survive and do the job you are expecting of it. Any weeds that are allowed to remain in the soil bed will haunt you for years to come. Before planting the ground cover is the easiest time to rid yourself of these unwanted guests. If left they will easily outgrow the freshly set out plants and smother them. When removing the weeds, be sure to get every bit of them, or new weeds will sprout up from old parts of a plant left behind in the soil.

You may want to spray the weeds with a kill-all weed killer a week to ten days before you loosen the soil. Usually this will solve the weed problem for you, except for the seeds that are waiting, ready to sprout when you begin watering your new ground-cover plants.

Prevention of seed germination can be handled two ways. After the new plants have been set in place, mulch the entire bed with two inches of peat moss. A mulch prevents the light and moisture from reaching the weed seeds. It also gives the new plants a chance to become established and capable of handling any minor competition from a few weedy plants that may find their way up through the mulch.

The second method is to use a preemergent weed killer that will kill the weedy seeds as they germinate. Be sure the chemical you select is labeled for use on the plants you have. If it isn't, there is a good chance the chemical will damage the ground cover, too.

PLANTING TIME

Ground covers can be set out just about any time of the year provided you give them adequate water to prevent the roots from drying out. There are certain times of the year when your chances of success are best. The type of plants you have selected and where you live determine the best time to set out your ground-cover material.

In the colder climates of the North, the earlier in the spring or summer you set out the plants the better are the odds that all of them will survive their first winter. The early planting insures that the roots will grow deep enough to get a firm grip on the soil and avoids the tearing apart of shallow roots with the winter freezing and thawing.

Deep-rooting plants may be planted in the early fall. They send down their roots quickly, so you won't have to worry about them over the winter months. Whether the plants are shallow or deep rooting, a one-inch or two-inch mulch over the ground will be very helpful. It prevents weeds, shades the new roots, and helps hold the moisture in the soil where the roots can absorb it.

DISTANCE BETWEEN NEW PLANTS VARIES

Spacing of the plants always presents a dilemma. You want the plants to cover the area quickly so you can enjoy the new look of your landscape, yet the cost of the plants is shocking. One way to get around the cost factor is to check with your friends and get several starts (cuttings) from their plants. This will require more work and time on your part, but you can save money and you'll get the satisfaction of growing your own plants. Later in Chapter 15 I'll discuss how to do your own propagation to increase your ground-cover beds.

Take into consideration the growing habit of the plants and how fast they spread. Size of the plants at the time you set them out will also govern how close together you place them. A single-stemmed plant will not fill in as quickly as a larger, more-developed one.

If spacing information is not included when you buy, be sure to inquire.

TO SUCCEED, WATER PROPERLY

Watering of the new plants is very important. The plants need water immediately after they have been set into the soil. All plants suffer shock when handled in the transplanting process, and a drink of water helps bring them out of it.

After the initial watering, plan on setting a sprinkler or hand-water every three or four days for two or three weeks. Don't drown the plants, but add just enough water to keep the soil slightly moist. As the plants become established and take hold in the soil, you can cut back on the amount of water you give them. Remember, they will need close watching during the first year after you have planted them. Don't neglect them!

14

How to Take Care of Your Ground Cover

Now that you have all the plants established and looking terrific, don't sit back to enjoy them and forget to take care of their needs. Ground-cover plants usually don't require much attention, but a few simple common sense maintenance procedures will perk them up and keep them looking well.

FERTILIZATION

Ground covers, like any other living things, need a continuous source of food. In this case we are talking about nitrogen, phosphorus, and potassium. The nitrogen produces a nice, green-colored plant; phosphorus is important in the formation of a healthy root system; and potassium performs in several ways, one of which is to help a plant ward off diseases.

The fertilizer you use should contain all three of these plant nutrients. Select a bag with an analysis of 10–10–10, 12–12–12, or 16–8–8. Apply 1½ to 2 pounds of one of these materials per 100 square feet of area. You will get the best results from this fertilization if you water immediately afterwards. Washing the plant food into the soil not only makes it more available to the plants but also prevents a chemical burn from occurring to the plants' delicate leaves.

Plant nutrients can be used whenever you feel there is a need for them. Usually an early spring or late fall application will be all the plants need. If you over fertilize and force the plants to grow too rapidly, you can do more harm to them than good.

WEED CONTROL

Don't let the weeds take over your ground cover! The idea was to create something unusual and beautiful in your yard—not a place where weeds predominate. Hand weeding, mulches, and chemical eradication are your three choices for a weed-free bed.

Annual weeds, such as shepherd's-purse, lamb's-quarters, and pigweed, can easily be pulled from the soil. Tackle this job after a light rain or watering has softened the soil. A few minutes each day on this task will keep these weeds under control.

The best solution is to use a two-inch layer of mulch over the soil to keep the weeds at a minimum. Just this much mulching material will prevent 90 percent of the possible weeds from ever getting started in your ground cover. Once the ground cover has spread over the area, only the most persistent weeds will be able to pop up through.

Control with preemergent chemicals offers a lot of possibilities. Check and recheck the label to be sure it is safe to use the material on your plants. If the plant isn't named specifically on the label, don't use the chemical. You're better off to hand-weed than to kill the ground cover along with the weeds.

Besides keeping the weeds out for the sake of appearance, you will be giving the desirable plants a better chance of developing a thick, lush cover. Competing weeds will slow down the growth of the ground cover and, if allowed to get completely out of control, will severely weaken them to the point where they never will fill in for you.

WATERING YOUR PLANTS

After the initial watering of the plants, you should keep them moist for a few weeks. Once the plants become established, they will not need as much water, but in droughty weather be sure to give them a drink.

An inch of water per week, either by rainfall or from a garden hose, will keep the plants in the best possible shape. Sure, they can get by with less water but then they won't look as healthy and often the leaf tips and leaf margins turn brown and curl up. This doesn't add much to the appearance of your landscape.

PRUNING GROUND COVER

Occasionally your ground-cover beds will get to looking ragged and in need of some kind of attention. Plants are growing in all directions—one sticking up here, another bent over there. A dead limb may be ruining the looks of the rest of the plants, or maybe an entire plant has died. Something needs to be done.

What can you do to tidy up? Simply get a pair of hand shears and start cutting out the slovenly plants. But, before starting, step back several feet and observe the overall appearance of the bed. Get a good picture of how you want it to look when you are through and then go to work. It's a good idea to step back from your work frequently to see if it is accomplishing what you set out to do in the beginning. You will want to remove all the dead plant material before seriously beginning the project.

Pruning can be very useful when you are first setting out the plants. Everyone hates to do it to a new plant because it makes it look smaller and because one thinks it will take longer for it to fill-in over to the next plant.

This is a mistaken idea, especially with the trailing-type and branching-type plants. When you cut off part of a stem, you allow the plant to use that portion of the plant's food to develop numerous lateral buds along the remaining stem. These buds will develop into a multi-stemmed plant that will eventually cover the ground more quickly than the original plant would have. Periwinkle, Baltic and English ivy, and wintercreeper are examples of ground-cover plants that benefit from being pruned at planting time. The cuttings may be rooted to increase your stock of plants if you wish to do so.

15

Propagating Your Own Ground-Cover Plants

After you have your ground-cover bed in and it is looking nice, you may wish to increase the size of the bed or start another one elsewhere in the yard. Instead of going to a nursery and buying the plants, why not start your own plants from the ones you already have? One of the biggest joys of gardening is propagating your own plants for use around the home.

There are several different techniques you can use to increase the number of plants you have. The one you use will be determined by the plants you have and your personal choice.

Keep in mind that each technique discussed will not work for every plant. You will need to check your plants and see how they are naturally increasing in size and numbers. A quick check with your local nursery will often supply the answer as to which propagating method to use.

LAYERING

Of all the ways to increase your plants, layering is the easiest. You merely take a limb that is trailing along the ground and cover it at each node with a little soil. In a matter of a few weeks new roots will have formed and you can separate the stem with its root system from the parent plant. Presto. You have another plant.

Select mature limbs for layering. They will produce roots faster than young stems. Usually one that is a year old is the best choice.

ROOT SEPARATION

This procedure is very similar to layering. Many of the trailing plants will send roots into the ground from each node on the plant that contacts the soil. Carpet bugle is one example of a plant propagated by this method.

How much more convenience could you ask for? All you have to do with these plants is sit back and enjoy them until it is time to start your new plants. Then you just snip off the rooted stems and set the plants in your new ground-cover beds.

STARTING FROM SEED

Many of the ground-cover plants can be started from seeds. It usually requires more work and takes longer to get a mature plant. The small ground-cover plants that are used around rocks, crevices, or cracks between rock walkways lend themselves to this type of propagation program.

The cost of seeds is very little and represents a considerable savings to you. The price of a single plant will buy several seed packets. Besides, growing plants from seed can be very rewarding. Don't hesitate to try it if you feel this is the best method for you and it fits your needs.

CUTTINGS

If you grow house plants, then you are probably familiar with increasing your plants by taking cuttings. You have probably taken broken plant parts or you have snipped a leaf from a favorite plant and put it into water to root. This is the simplest kind of cutting. It works well if you are working with a few cuttings, but when you are getting ready to start a new ground-cover bed you will need fifty to one thousand plants. Placing this many in water to root is not very convenient.

The best way to handle rooting of a large number of plants is to use a special mixture of soil and organic materials. This will enable you to prepare a rooting bed for your cuttings with just the right amount of water and air to enable the roots to develop rapidly and healthily.

Your pre-mix rooting soil should be composed of 80 percent

organic material (peat moss, leafmold, compost) and 20 percent mineral matter. A sandy, loose soil should account for half of the mineral matter, with calcine clay, perlite, or vermiculite making up the other half.

Take your cuttings from the tips of the plants; this will give you young plant material, the cells of which still have rapid rejuvenation powers. Older material can be used but with less success and a longer waiting period for the roots to form.

Length of the cuttings should be from 4 inches to 6 inches long when possible. Strip the leaves from the lower 2 to 3 inches of the cutting. With a razor blade, scissors, or sharp knife, make a diagonal cut across the stem just below a node. This exposes more stem surface than cutting straight across.

Next, place the cutting in your prepared rooting mix. Push the stems into the soil two to three inches and hand-pack the soil around the cutting. Keep the mixture moist but not soggy until the new roots form. When they have grown to one to two inches in length and have branched off, forming lateral roots, you can transplant them. Treat them gently during the transplanting as they are still very sensitive to changes at this stage of their development. Give them a good drink of water immediately after you have finished transplanting.

Five very good examples of plants that may be started from cuttings are Baltic and English ivy, pachysandra, wintercreeper, and periwinkle.

16

Selecting Ground Covers for Your Landscape

So far you have learned the value of using ground covers and how they add that extra something to your landscape. The proper steps to take to prepare your soil for planting have been given to you. Maintenance requirements of the plants have been discussed, along with how to increase the number of plants you have by using the correct propagation technique. Now it's time to look into the selection of the ground covers and the different types of plants available.

The United States Department of Agriculture has developed a plant-hardiness map you will find very useful when deciding what ground cover to plant. The map is divided into 10 zones, each

Ground-Cover Hardiness-Zone Map

Zone 1	Below −50°F	Zone 6	−10° to 0°
Zone 2	−50° to −40°	Zone 7	0° to 10°
Zone 3	−40° to −30°	Zone 8	10° to 20°
Zone 4	−30° to −20°	Zone 9	20° to 30°
Zone 5	−20° to −10°	Zone 10	30° to 40°

one representing a definite climatic region. These zones are determined by the average minimum winter temperatures in each zone.

Let's look at the map, pick out a plant, and see how to determine where it is adapted for use. Selecting the very popular English ivy, and from the tables in this chapter listing various ground covers and their zone of adaptation, we find it is listed in zone 5.

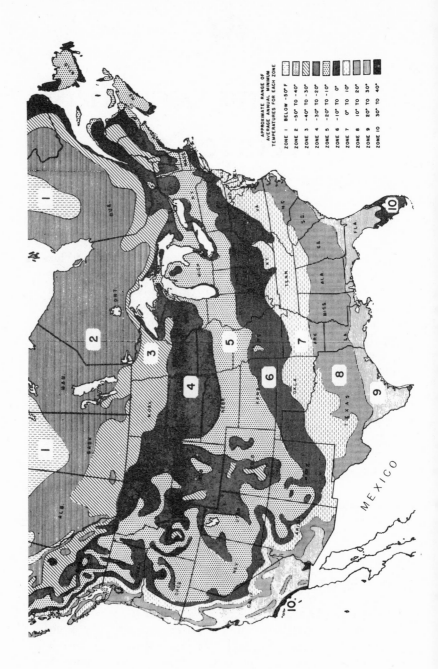

APPROXIMATE RANGE OF
AVERAGE ANNUAL MINIMUM
TEMPERATURES FOR EACH ZONE

ZONE 1   BELOW -50° F
ZONE 2   -50° TO -40°
ZONE 3   -40° TO -30°
ZONE 4   -30° TO -20°
ZONE 5   -20° TO -10°
ZONE 6   -10° TO 0°
ZONE 7   0° TO 10°
ZONE 8   10° TO 20°
ZONE 9   20° TO 30°
ZONE 10   30° TO 40°

MEXICO

This plant can then be grown with almost complete certainty anywhere in zone 5 on the map.

If you try to grow it in zone 4, where annual minimum temperatures are colder, there is not much of a chance the plant will survive the winter weather. A local climatic condition may exist in zone 4 that would permit English ivy to grow, but this would be an isolated exception to the rule. This is not all that uncommon, especially if the plant is protected from the harsh winter weather by some sort of barrier or shelter.

Before trying to grow a plant in a zone north of where it is adapted, check around the garden centers and nurseries to see if they sell the plant. If it is not available, then you have a good indication of whether it will survive in your yard.

English ivy may be grown anywhere south of zone 5 without worrying about it. As a general rule of thumb, then, when using the plant-hardiness map, you can grow plants south of the zone of adaptation they are listed in. Plant adaptation southward is limited by the summer's heat or droughty conditions instead of the cold winter temperatures that restrict its growth northward. Occasionally plants may be grown one zone north of their zone of adaptation, but this will be determined by individual instances where some unusual feature of the area protects the plants from cold temperatures in that zone.

Remember, the smaller the zone number, the lower the winter temperatures. Thus, a plant able to withstand a certain amount of coolness cannot advance beyond its zone of adaptation and have a very good chance of survival. Buying a zone 5 plant and trying to grow it in zone 3 or 4 is usually a waste of your time and money. Use the plant-hardiness map and your chances of success are greatly improved, provided you give the plants the proper attention they need to be healthy and vigorous.

TABLE 16–1

Ground-Covers Area of Adaptation

ZONE 1	Bluets	Dwarf anchusa
		Sea thrift
ZONE 2	Beach wormwood	Bunchberry
	Bearberry	Creeping phlox
	Bloodroot	Creeping snowberry

Ground-Covers Area of Adaptation (Continued)

Daylily
Fringed bleeding-heart
Gill-over-the-ground
Lily-of-the-valley
Moss pink
Moss sandwort
Mother-of-thyme

Mugo pine
Pinks
Shore juniper
Trillium
Violets
Wintergreen
Wooly yarrow

ZONE 3

Aubretia
Beach strawberry
Bishop's goutweed
Blue fescue
Camomile
Cinquefoil
Creeping baby's-breath
Crown vetch
Dwarf blueflowers
Harebell

Mock strawberry
Lungwort
Moneywort
Plantain-lily
Pussytoes
Periwinkle
Rugosa rose
Silver mound artemisia
Speedwell
Stone cress

ZONE 4

Bergenia
Bird's-foot trefoil
Carpet bugle
Coral bells
Dead nettle
Evergreen candytuft
Foam flower
Germander
Gold dust

Heathers
Hens-and-chickens
Japanese spurge
Lady's-mantle
Oregon grape
Primrose
Sand myrtle
Saxifrage
Wintercreeper

ZONE 5

Bearberry cotoneaster
Blue leadwort
Broom
Creeping mint
English ivy
Hall's honeysuckle
Jewel mint
Iceplant

Kenilworth ivy
Lamb's ears
Lily turf
Mazus
Mondo grass
Pachistima
Sarcococca
Savory
Virginia creeper

ZONE 6

Carolina jasmine
Kudsu vine
New Zealand bur

Strawberry begonia
White cup
Wire vine

ZONE 7	Baby's tears	Hooker Manzanita
	Carmel creeper	Ivy geranium
	Dichondra	Lantana
	Dwarf rosemary	Laurel hill manzanita
	Ground morning glory	Mat grass
		Star jasmine

ZONES 8, 9, and 10   Most of the plants listed under the other zones are adapted for use in zones 8, 9, and 10. Some of the more reliable ones are carpet bugle, Carolina jasmine, daylily, dicondra, English ivy, ferns, iceplant, lilyturf, periwinkle, star jasmine, wandering jew, and wintercreeper.

TABLE 16–2

Choose Your Shade-Tolerant Plants from This List

Asparagus fern	Mazus
Australian bluebell	Mock strawberry
Baby's tears	Mondo grass
Bearberry	Moss sandwort
Bearberry cotoneaster	Oregon grape
Bloodroot	Periwinkle
Carpet bugle	Sand myrtle
Bluets	Sarcococca
Coral bells	Saxifrage
Dicondra	Star jasmine
Dwarf blueflowers	Strawberry begonia
Dwarf Chinese holly	Trillium
English ivy	Violets
Gill-over-the-ground	Virginia creeper
Japanese spurge	Wintercreeper
Lily-of-the-valley	Wintergreen
Lily turf	

Fifteen Ground Covers That Stay Green Year Round

Bearberry	Japanese spurge
Bearberry cotoneaster	Mother-of-thyme
Broom	Oregon grape
Canby pachistima	Periwinkle
English ivy	Sarcococca
Hall's honeysuckle	Wineleaf cinquefoil
Heathers	Wintercreeper
Heaths	

Choose Your Shade-Tolerant Plants from This List (Continued)

Plants That Do Well in Acid Soils

Aubretia	Hall's honeysuckle
Bearberry	Japanese spurge
Bergenia	Lamb's ears
Bishop's goutweed	Lily-turf
Bluets	Mother-of-thyme
Broom	Pachistima
Carpet bugle	Periwinkle
Cinquefoil	Plantain-lily
Creeping phlox	Trillium
Crown vetch	Wintercreeper
English ivy	Wintergreen

Ten Quick-Spreading Ground Covers

Bishop's goutweed	Mazus
Broom	Mother-of-thyme
Carpet bugle	Lily-of-the-valley
English ivy	Periwinkle
Japanese spurge	Wintercreeper

Plants for the Seaside

Beach strawberry	Lily-turf
Beach wormwood	Moss sandwort
Blue fescue	Mugo pine
Creeping baby's-breath	Rugosa rose
Crimson jewel	Sea thrift
Dwarf rosemary	Shore juniper
Heathers	Silver yarrow
Heaths	Wire plant
Iceplant	

Plants for Rock Walkways, Flagstone Steps and Patios

	Tolerates Foot Traffic	Aesthetic Value Only	Fragrant When Stepped On
Baby's tears	X		
Bluets	X		
Blue fescue		X	
Camomile	X		X
Creeping baby's-breath		X	
Dwarf rosemary		X	X

Jewel mint	X		X
Mazus	X		
Moneywort		X	
Moss pink		X	
Moss sandwort	X		
Mother-of-thyme	X		X
Pinks		X	
Pussytoes	X		
Sea thrift		X	
Speedwell	X		
Wooly yarrow	X		X

Plants Requiring Well-Drained Soils

Blue fescue	Heaths
Coral bells	Hens-and-chickens
Creeping baby's-breath	Lamb's-ears
Dwarf rosemary	Lantana
Evergreen candytuft	Mother-of-thyme
Fringed bleeding-heart	Moss sandwort
Germander	Pinks
Gold Dust	Saxifrage
Harebell	Sea thrift
Heathers	

Plants for Rock Gardens and Crevices

Aubretia	Ivy geranium
Bearberry cotoneaster	Kenilworth ivy
Bergenia	Lamb's-ears
Blue leadwort	Pinks
Bluets	Sand myrtle
Carpet bugle	Savory
Creeping baby's-breath	Sea thrift
Creeping mint	Silver mound artemisia
Gold Dust	Speedwell
Heathers	Stone cress
Hens-and-chickens	

GROUND COVERS AND THEIR MANY NAMES

Often a single plant may have several common names. This can be very misleading and confusing to gardeners when they are trying to buy a particular ground-cover plant. To help solve this dilemma for you, I have compiled the following list of plants and alphabetically listed them by their scientific names. Following each are as many of their common names as I could find in use around the country. Using the scientific name is the best way to be certain you are getting the plant you want from a nursery or garden center.

TABLE 16-3

Scientific Name	Common Name
Acaena microphylla	New Zealand bur
Achillea argentea	Silver yarrow
Achillea tomentosa	Wooly yarrow
Aegopodium podogravia	Bishop's goutweed
	Goutweed
	Silver edge Bishop's weed
	Silver edge goatweed
Aethionema warleyense	Persian candytuft
	Stone cress
Ajuga reptans	Bugleweed
	Carpet bugle
Alchemilla vulgaris	Lady's mantle
Allyssum saxatile	Basket-of-gold
	Golden tuft
	Gold Dust
Antennaria rosea	Pussytoes
Anthemis nobilis	Camomile
	Chamomile
	English chamomile
	Roman chamomile
Arctostaphylos franciscana	Laurel hill manzanita
Arctostaphylos hookeri	Hooker manzanita
Arctostaphylos uva-ursi	Bearberry
	Kinnikinnick
Arenaria verna	Iris moss
	Lazy-man's lawn
	Moss sandwort
Armeria maritima	Sea thrift
	Thrift
	Common thrift
	Sea pink
Artemisia schmidtiana	Silver mound artemisia
	Satiny wormwood

Artemisia stelleriana	Beach wormwood
	Dusty-miller
Asparagus sprengerii	Asparagus fern
	Sprenger asparagus
Aubretia deltoides	Aubretia
Bergenia cordifolia	Bergenia
	Saxifrage
	Megasea
Bergenia crassifolia	Saxifrage
	Siberian tea
	Winter blooming bergenia
	Leather bergenia
Bougainvillea species	Crimson jewel
Brunnera macrophylla	Dwarf anchusa
Calluna species	Heathers
Campanula partenshlagiana	Harebell
	Dwarf blueflowers
	Tussock bell flowers
Ceanothus griseus	Carmel creeper
Ceratostigma plumbaginoides	Blue leadwort
	Blue certostigma
Convallaria majalis	Lily-of-the-valley
Convolunlus mauritanicus	Ground morning glory
Cornus canadensis	Bunchberry
	Dwarf cornel
Coronilla varia	Crown vetch
Cotoneaster dammari	Bearberry cotoneaster
Cymbalaria muralis	Kenilworth ivy
Cytisus species	Broom
Dianthus species	Pinks
	Gorden Pinks
Dicentra eximia	Fringed bleeding-heart
Dichondra repens	Dichondra
	Lawn leaf
	Pony foot
Duchesnea indica	Mock strawberry
	Indian strawberry
Erica species	Heaths
Euonymus fortunei	Wintercreeper
Festuca ovina	Blue fescue
Fragaria chiloensis	Beach strawberry
	Sand strawberry
	Wild strawberry
Gaultheria hispidula	Creeping snowberry

TABLE 16–3 (*Continued*)

Scientific Name	Common Name
Gaultheria species	Creeping pearlberry
	Wintergreen
	Checkerberry
	Teaberry
Gelsemium sempervirens	Carolina jasmine
Glecoma hederacea	Gill-over-the-ground
Gypsophila repens	Creeping baby's-breath
	Creeping gypsophila
Hedera helix	English ivy
Helxine solierolii	Baby's-tears
	Angel-tears
Hemercocallis species	Daylily
Heuchera sanquinea	Coral bells
Hosta species	Plantain-lily
Houstonia caeralea	Bluets
	Quaker ladies
Hypericum moserianum	Gold-flower
Iberis sempervirens	Evergreen candytuft
	Candytuft
Ilex cornuta	Dwarf Chinese holly
Juniperus conferta	Shore juniper
Lamium maculatum	Dead nettle
	Spotted dead nettle
Lantana montevidensis	Lantana
	Trailing lantana
	Weeping lantana
Leiophyllum buxifolium	Sand myrtle
	Box sand myrtle
Lippia canescens	Mat grass
Liriope spicata	Lily-turf
	Creeping lily-turf
Lonicera japonica	Hall's honeysuckle
Lotus corniculatus	Bird's-foot trefoil
	Ground honeysuckle
	Baby's-slippers
	Bloom-fell
Lysimachia nummularia	Moneywort
	Creeping Jennie
	Creeping Charlie

Mahonia aquifolium	Oregon grape
	Oregon holly-grape
Mazus reptans	Mazus
	Creeping mazus
Mentha requienii	Jewel mint
	Creeping mint
	Jewel mint of Corsica
	Corsican mint
Mesembryanthemum species	Iceplant
	Fig-marigold
Muehlenbeckia complexa	Wire plant
	Maidenhair vine
	Mattress-vine
Nierembergia rivularis	White cup
Ophiopogon japonicas	Mondo grass
	Dwarf lily-turf
Pachistima canbyi	Pachistima
	Dwarf hedge
	Canby pachistima
	Rat-stripper
Pachysandra terminalis	Pachysandra
	Japanese spurge
	Japanese pachysandra
Parthenocissus quinquefolia	Virginia creeper
	American ivy
	Woodbine
Pelargonium peltatum	Ivy geranium
Phlox subulata	Creeping phlox
	Moss pink
	Ground pink
	Mountain pink
	Moss phlox
Pinus mugo	Mugo pine
	Mountain pine
Potentilla tridentata	Cinquefoil
	Wineleaf cinquefoil
	Three-toothed cinquefoil
Primula species	Primrose
Pueraria thunbergiana	Kudsu vine
	Kudzu vine
Pulmonaria soccarata	Lungwort
	Bethlehem sage
Rosa rugosa	Rugosa rose
Rosmarinus officinalis	Dwarf rosemary

TABLE 16–3 (*Continued*)

Scientific Name	Common Name
Sanguinaria canadensis	Bloodroot
Sarcococca humilis	Sarcococca
	Sweet-box
Satureia species	Savory
Saxifraga sarmentosa	Strawberry
	Strawberry geranium
	Strawberry begonia
	Mother-of-thousands
Sempervivum tectorum	Hens-and-chickens
	Houseleek
	Sempervivum
Sollya heterophylla	Australian bluebell
Stachys lanata	Lamb's-ears
	Lamb's-tongue
	Wooly betony
Teucrium chamaedrys	Germander
Thymus serphyllum	Mother-of-thyme
	Creeping thyme
Tiarella cordifolia	Foam flowers
	False mitre-wort
	Coolwort
	Alleghany foam-flower
Trachelospermum jasminoides	Star jasmine
	Confederate jasmine
Trillium species	Trillium
	Wakerobins
Veronica repens	Speedwell
	Veronica
	Creeping speedwell
Vinca minor	Periwinkle
	Myrtle
	Creeping myrtle
Viola species	Violets

TABLE 16-4
Some Herbs Used as Ground Covers

Scientific Name	Common Name	Zone	Flower Color	Exposure	Comments
Achillea millefolium	Yarrow	2	yellow	sun	Pungent, finely divided, fernlike leaves.
Allium schoenoprasum	Chives	2	lavender	sun, shade	Grass-like aromatic foliage.
Anthemis nobilis	Chamomile	3	yellow	sun	Finely cut, bright green leaves.
Artemesia ludoviciana 'albula'	Silver king	2	yellow, white	sun	Decorative silvery foliage.
Asperula odorata	Sweet woodruff	4	white	shade	Leaves in whorls.
Gaultheria spp.	Wintergreen	2	white	shade	Bright red fruit; source of oil.
Rosmarinus officinalis prostratus	Rosemary	7	blue	sun	Needle-like gray foliage.
Santolina chamaecyparissus	Lavender cotton	5	yellow	sun	Pungent silver-gray foliage.
Satureja montana pygaea	Winter savory	5	lavender	sun	Aromatic leaves.
Stachys olympica	Wooly betony	5	reddish purple	sun	Gray wooly foliage; good edging.
Teucrium chamaedrys	Germander	4	lavender	sun or lt. shade	Small glossy leaves.

Reprinted with the permission of Rain Bird Sprinkler Manufacturing Corporation.

TABLE 16-5

Ground Covers for Slopes and Lawn Substitutes

Name	Flower Color	Growth Rate	Exposure	Area	Comments
Abelia grandiflora prostrata Prostrate abelia	white	moderate	sun, part shade	any	New growth reddish, turning shiny green. Under trees and on slopes.
Acacia longifolia Golden acacia	yellow	fast	sun	large	Mass of foliage and flowers to 20 ft. Holds soil on slopes.
Achillea argentea Silvery yarrow	yellow	fast	sun	small	Silver gray leaves 3-6 in. high; good for lawn or patterns.
A. tomentosa Wooly yarrow	yellow	fast	sun	any	Accepts hot dry location and poor soil. Good lawn substitute.
Ajuga reptans Carpet bugle	blue	fast	part shade	small	Many varieties with leaves large and small; bronze; varigated; versatile.
Alternanthera bettzickiana Telanthera	nonblooming	fast	sun	small	Red or green foliage; excellent for pattern planting.
Anthemis nobilis Chamomile	yellow	moderate	sun	small	Fine-cut, moss-like foliage aromatic when stepped on; excellent lawn substitute.

Ground Covers for Slopes and Lawn Substitutes (Continued)

Name	Flower Color	Growth Rate	Exposure	Area	Comments
Arctostaphylos uva-ursi Bearberry	white	slow	sun, shade	large	Spreads to 10-12 ft.; fruit red; use on slopes and under trees.
Arenaria verna caespitosa Irish moss	white	moderate	sun	small	Moss-like plant for sunny areas; can be walked on.
Armeria maratima Sea thrift	pink	moderate	sun	small	Grows in grassy clumps; fine lawn substitute.
Asparagus sprengeri Asparagus fern	white	moderate	sun, shade	small	Red berries; use under trees and for inaccessible areas.
Baccharis pilularis Dwarf coyote bush	white or yellow	fast	sun	large	Light green foliage; strong roots; little water; good for slopes or wild areas.
Bergenia crassifolia Saxifrage	pink	moderate	shade	small	Large leaves for shade area under trees; winter-blooming.
Bougainvillea 'Crimson Jewel'	crimson	fast	sun	any	Bush type ideal in hard-to-water areas; color accent.
Callistemon phoeniceus Prostrate bottlebrush	red	fast	sun	large	Flower brushes to 4 in. long; good on slopes.

Ground Covers for Slopes and Lawn Substitutes (Continued)

Name	Flower Color	Growth Rate	Exposure	Area	Comments
Campanula portenschlagiana Dalmation bellflower	blue	slow	shade	small	Tidy, compact and spreading; flowers from May to July; grows under trees.
Carissa grandiflora horizontalis Creeping natal plum	white	fast	sun	large	Armoured with piercing thorns; protects property; shiny green foliage.
Cerastium tomentosum Snow-in-summer	white	fast	sun	large	Contrasts pleasingly with green covers for lawn substitute and for patterns.
Convolvulus cineorum Bush morning glory	white	fast	sun	small	Not an invader like weeds of the same name; colorful pattern.
C. mauriticus Ground morning glory	blue	fast	sun	large	Plant on 3-foot centers on either slopes or flat areas.
Cotoneaster dammari Bearberry cotoneaster	white	moderate	sun, shade	large	Flattest growing; spreads widely; rock and slopes.
Cytisus kewensis Scotch broom	white	fast	sun	large	Spreads 3-4 feet; slopes and wild areas.

Ground Covers for Slopes and Lawn Substitutes (Continued)

Name	Flower Color	Growth Rate	Exposure	Area	Comments
Dianthus spp. Pinks	pink, red	fast	sun	small	Flowers fragrant; thrives in rocky soil; lawn substitute; patterns.
Dichondra repens Dichondra	nonblooming	fast	sun, shade	large	Best substitute for grass in California; large lawn areas.
Duchesnea indica Mock strawberry	yellow	fast	part shade	large	Good for wild areas that are watered often; also on slopes and flat places.
Festina ovina glauca Blue fescue	nonblooming	fast	sun, part shade	small	Blue-green foliage; ideal for creating interesting patterns.
Fragaria chiloensis Beach strawberry	white	fast	sun, part shade	small	Cultivated variety, No. 25 also gives edible fruit; use on slopes or flat areas.
Gazania splendens Gazania	yellow, red, pink, white, orange	moderate	sun	small	Gray foliage; good for parking strips; colorful lawn substitute.
G. uniflora Trailing gazania	yellow, white, orange	fast	sun	any	Blooms profusely; grows well in relatively poor soil; ideal for slopes.
Glecoma hederacea Gill-over-the-ground	purple	fast	shade	medium	Needs moisture; very weedy; lawn substitute for poor soil.

Ground Covers for Slopes and Lawn Substitutes (Continued)

Name	Flower Color	Growth Rate	Exposure	Area	Comments
Gypsophila repens Creeping baby's-breath	white	fast	sun	small	Silvery foliage; needs well-drained soil; substitute for grass lawn.
Hedera canariensis Algerian ivy	nonblooming	fast	sun, shade	any	Leaves large, dark green; most popular ground-cover in adapted areas.
Helianthemum nummularium Sunrose	many vivid colors	fast	sun	medium	Low-growing mass of leaves and stems; large, 2" flowers; slopes or flat areas.
Helxine solierolii Baby's tears	nonblooming	fast	shade	small	Useful as lawn substitute in deep shade; living mulch.
Heuchera sanguinea Coral bells	pink	slow	sun, part shade	small	Evergreen; myriads of tiny flowers on long stalks; slopes or lawn substitute.
Hypericum calycinum Aaron's beard	yellow	fast	part shade	large	Yellow-green foliage; spreads by underground runners; slopes, flat areas.
H. repens St. John's wort	yellow	fast	sun	small	Thick, low carpet studded with tiny flowers; good substitute for grass lawn.

Ground Covers for Slopes and Lawn Substitutes (Continued)

Name	Flower Color	Growth Rate	Exposure	Area	Comments
Iberis sempervirens Evergreen candytuft	white	slow	sun	small	Dark green foliage; good all year; slopes and level areas.
Ilex cornuta burfordi Dwarf Chinese holly	white	slow	shade	small	Compact, shiny leaves; good for shade areas; patterns.
Lantana sellowiana Trailing lantana	lavender	fast	sun	large	Many semi-trailing varieties; varied colors; ideal for slopes.
Lippia repens Mat grass	lilac	fast	sun	small	Good for hot locations; excellent substitute for grass lawn.
Liriope spicata Lily turf	white or blue	slow	sun, shade	small	Fountain of dark green, narrow, 18″ leaves; fruit dark blue; lawn substitute.
Lonicera japonica halliana Hall's honeysuckle	white, yellow	fast	sun, part shade	large	Extremely vigorous; needs room to grow; slopes and wild areas.
Lotus berthelotii Parrot's beak	red	fast	sun	any	Feathery gray foliage; slopes and patterns.
Lysimachia nummularia Moneywort	yellow	fast	sun, shade	medium	Needs moisture; weedy; lawn substitute.

Ground Covers for Slopes and Lawn Substitutes (*Continued*)

Name	Flower Color	Growth Rate	Exposure	Area	Comments
Mahonia aquifolium Oregon grape	yellow	slow	sun, shade	large	Bronze foliage when young; fall red leaves; bluish berries; slopes, under trees.
Mazus reptans Mazus	blue	moderate	sun, shade	small	Needs plenty of moisture; lawn substitute and pattern planting.
Mentha requienii Jewel mint	purple	moderate	sun	small	Flat like moss; fragrant when crushed; lawn substitute; between stepping stones.
Mesembryanthemum spp. Iceplant	varied	fast	sun	any	Varied group; adapts to sterile soil, little or no water; colorful on slopes or level.
Muehlenbeckia complexa Wire vine	nonblooming	fast	sun	large	Small leaves; best for beach planting; holds sand; slopes.
Ophiopogon japonicum Mondo grass	white	slow	sun, shade	any	Forms a sod; grows almost anywhere; lawn substitute.
Pachsyandra terminalis Japanese spurge	white	fast	shade	large	Evergreen; ideal under trees and on slopes; acid soil; handsome leaves.
Pelargonium peltatum Ivy geranium	varied	fast	part shade	any	Trailing, with white, pink, red, lavender blooms; slopes and level areas.

Ground Covers for Slopes and Lawn Substitutes (Continued)

Name	Flower Color	Growth Rate	Exposure	Area	Comments
Plumbago capense Leadwort	blue	fast	sun	large	Profuse phlox-like flowers in summer; slopes and wild areas.
Polygonum capitatum Pink knotweed	pink	fast	sun, part shade	any	Very tender to frost; lawn substitute and on slopes.
Potentilla cinerea Cinquefoil	yellow	fast	sun, shade	any	Good-looking strawberry-like leaves; easy, adapts to poor soil; slopes or lawn.
Pyracantha crenatoserrata 'Santa Cruz'	white	fast	sun	large	Red berries are attractive; good for slopes.
Rosemarinus officinalis Santa Barbara rosemary	light blue	slow	sun	any	Aromatic foliage; ideal for dry banks near ocean; slopes.
Sagina subulata Scotch moss	white	moderate	sun	small	Chartreuse moss for hot, sunny place; patterns; lawn substitute.
Santolina chamacyparissus Lavender cotton	yellow	fast	sun	large	Evergreen aromatic foliage; finely divided gray leaves; wild areas, slopes.
Saxifraga sarmentosa Strawberry begonia	white	fast	shade	small	Useful for under trees and for patterns.

Ground Covers for Slopes and Lawn Substitutes (Continued)

Name	Flower Color	Growth Rate	Exposure	Area	Comments
Sollya heterophylla Australian bluebell	blue	moderate	shade	medium	Ideal under eucalyptus trees; slopes and flat areas.
Stachys lanata Lamb's ears	purple	fast	sun	small	Spreads 2-3 feet; should be cut back in winter; distinctive leaves.
Trachelospermum jasminoides Star jasmine	white	slow	part shade	any	Outstanding for fragrance; slopes and shaded level areas.
Verbena peruviana Verbena	red, pink, white	fast	sun	large	Needs mowing each year; dazzling blooms most of year; slopes and level.
Veronica repens Veronica Speedwell	blue	fast	sun, part shade	medium	Weedy; useful as paving plant between flagstones; ideal lawn substitute.
Vinca minor Periwinkle	blue	fast	part shade	large	Grows in almost impossible soil, exposure; slopes and under trees.
Wedelia trilobata Wedelia	yellow	fast	sun	large	Leaves leathery, dark green; flowers most of year; slopes and lawn substitute.

Reprinted with the permission of Rain Bird Sprinkler Manufacturing Corporation.

17

Frequently Asked Questions About Ground Covers, and Their Answers

370. *What is a ground cover?*

The definition of a ground cover can be stated simply as the use of any plant that spreads over the soil, protecting it from erosion by wind and rain. To be used as a landscaping plant, it must be aesthetically pleasing, quick spreading, and easy to maintain.

371. *Why are the fancy Latin terms usually given along with the common household names of the ground covers?*

Ground-cover plants are some of the worst offenders when it comes to having multiple common names. One plant is reported to have more than 25 common names, each depending on the area where it is found growing.

As an example, it can be very confusing when trying to buy a ground-cover plant if you ask for creeping phlox and the nursery has it labeled as moss pink or creeping pink or ground pink or mountain pink. Had you known the Latin name, *Phlox sublata*, you could have avoided this problem.

Consider the ground cover *Lysimachia nummularia*, which comes under a variety of names. Some of these are moneywort, creeping Charlie, and creeping Jennie.

Although it isn't necessary to memorize these somewhat awkward Latin names, it is a good idea to have them written down on a piece of paper when you go to the garden center. Check the table in Chapter 16 that lists the Latin (scientific) name and the various common names for each plant. Often the Latin name is included on the name tag of a plant and you can check it with yours to be sure you are buying the plant you want.

372. Does a ground cover eliminate maintenance altogether?

No. Ground covers make the job of maintaining your garden areas easier, but they can't be totally ignored or you will end up with a lot of weeds.

Keeping the weeds out, occasionally fertilizing, watering during dry spells, cleaning trash from the plants, and watching for any insect problems generally make up the list of jobs you'll have to perform—substantially less work than you have to do keep your lawn looking nice.

373. I am planning on adding some ground cover to the landscape around my home. When is the best time to begin setting the plants in the ground?

An exact date is impossible to predict because of varying weather conditions around the country and differences in individual plant requirements.

As a general rule you can plant ground cover any time, but there are certain times that are better than others. For example, spring plantings are best because the plant has a full growing season to become established before the winter months arrive.

You may plant in the fall but do it in the first half of the season. Allow six weeks of good growing weather so the plants can get a healthy start before cold weather sets in on them.

If you are like most gardeners, spring is a very busy time of the year. There is so much work to do, it is impossible to get everything accomplished. For this reason you may wish to wait until late spring or even early summer to start your ground-cover plants. Watering them thoroughly through the summer is essential if the plants are to do well at all.

Checking the local conditions and using good common sense will allow you to decide the best planting time for you and your plants.

374. What is the best spacing between plants?

This depends upon the types of plants you are going to use and how quickly you want them to cover.

Plants such as ajuga and pachysandra should not be set any closer than six inches, while a spacing of one foot would be maximum. Also at the one-foot spacing are the alpine and clump plants used around rocky areas of a garden. Shrubs such as cotoneaster and junipers should be spaced at three-foot intervals. Larger-spreading plants, such as rock cotoneaster, may be a little farther apart because of the way their growth spreads out.

As you can see, the type of plant you use will really determine the spacing. This information should be available at the nursery where you buy the plants. (See Table 17–1.)

TABLE 17–1

Ground-Cover	Distance Between Plants When Setting Them Out (inches)
Bird's-foot trefoil	6
Blue leadwort	18 to 24
Bunchberry	12
Camomile	12
Creeping Phlox	12 to 18
Dwarf rosemary	24
Foam flowers	12
Germander	24
Jewel mint	6
Lamb's-ears	18
Lantana	18
Lily-turf	12
Lily-of-the-valley	9 to 12
Mondo grass	6
Moneywort	12 to 18
Mother-of-thyme	6 to 12
Pachysandra	6 to 12
Periwinkle	18
Speedwell	6 to 12
Star jasmine	30 to 36
Strawberry geranium	8 to 9

375. Could you give me some idea of the number of plants I will need to cover a large ground-cover bed?

The first step is to determine the number of square feet you have. Next select the ground cover that does well in your area. The local nurseries should be able to tell you the number of plants needed to cover your bed. (See Table 17–2.)

The more plants you use, the quicker the ground will become

TABLE 17-2

Fifteen Ground Covers and Number of Plants Needed to Cover a One-Thousand Foot Area

Ground Covers	Plants
Ajuga	2,000 to 2,500
Blue leadwort	350 to 500
Bunchberry	850 to 950
Camomile	900 to 1,000
Dwarf rosemary	450 to 500
Honeysuckle	300 to 400
Ivy	400 to 500
Jewel mint	1,700 to 1,800
Lily-of-the-valley	800 to 1,300
Lily-turf	1,000 to 1,300
Moneywort	1,000 to 1,200
Pachysandra	1,000 to 2,000
Periwinkle	900 to 1,000
Sarcococca	650 to 800
Wintercreeper	800 to 900

covered. Cost of the plants will usually restrict the number of plants you buy to the minimum number needed to get the job done.

376. What are some good mulching materials?

The list of mulching materials is limited by what is available in your area, by your imagination, and by the cost of the materials. Check around the neighborhood and see what everyone else is using before settling on one for your use. Be imaginative and select one that does the job and adds a touch of elegance to your particular landscape.

Partial List of Mulching Materials

Bark chips	Peat moss
Black plastic	Pine needles
Black tar paper	Seed hulls (buckwheat)
Crushed tile or brick	Small pebbles
Decorative rocks	Straw
Ground corncobs	Washed gravel
Landscape stones	Wood chips

377. What exactly does a mulch accomplish when used in a ground-cover bed?

Mulches accomplish several things for you and your plants. The appearance of a ground-cover bed is greatly enhanced by the proper use of a mulch.

A mulch helps to trap the water in the ground, storing it, and allowing for better plant growth. Weeds are less of a problem, since they have a difficult time growing up through the mulch and a layer of ground-cover plants.

378. Each winter it seems that more of my ground-cover plants are injured. Some even die. How can I protect my plants from this problem with which I seem plagued?

Damage to the plants in the winter is caused by a combination of the sun glaring down on the plants, a cold wind blowing over the leaves, and frigid temperatures. Anything you can do to protect your plants from these three elements will prevent damage.

If you have a snow cover over the plants most of the winter, you should not see as many injured plants in the spring. Snow is an excellent insulator and protects the plants well. A mulch of straw or evergreen boughs will do the job too.

379. I have seen the words acid, sweet, and pH frequently when reading about ground covers. Just what do these words refer to?

These terms are all used when talking about the soil where the plant's roots must live. The designation pH is used in explaining whether the soil's chemical reaction is acid (sour) or alkaline (sweet).

If it is acid, there is a lot of hydrogen present in the soil; if alkaline, then calcium and magnesium predominate over any hydrogen present. A third term, saline, refers to a soil that has large quantities of sodium in it. Saline soils often occur in potted house plants if the water being used had been passed through a soft-water conditioner.

A scale of 1 through 14 is used in testing pH. Acid soils are 1 to 7, and alkaline soils are 7 to 14. An even 7 is said to be a neutral soil. Most plants prefer a pH in the range of 6.0 to 7.5.

380. A friend has told me how much better my plants will do if I add lime to the soil. Is lime a fertilizer?

Lime is usually not thought of as a fertilizer. It does, however, contain calcium and magnesium, which are two important plant foods.

When the soil is acid (pH below 7), then lime is used to change it and make the soil more suitable for good plant growth. Lime comes in different forms. Usually a finely ground lime is best and will do a good job for you. Hydrated lime should be used only where there is a need for a quick change in the soil's condition.

Don't apply any lime until you have had a soil test to determine it is needed. Basically the lime does five things for a plant. It supplies both calcium and magnesium, raises the pH, aids in the decomposition of organic matter, makes other nutrients in the soil more available to the plants, and makes a soil more open and loose.

381. Can I add sand to the soil to improve it?

You can, but I don't recommend it unless you are going to haul in enough to do the job properly. It takes a tremendous amount of sand to improve a soil, especially if it is high in clay.

For the amount of money you will spend for sand, you could buy some organic material and do a much better job in improving the soil. Sand just doesn't add much, whereas the benefits of organic material are numerous. It granulates the soil, adds food for both plants and soil organisms, holds moisture, and improves the overall condition of the soil.

382. Are there any good ground-cover plants that will grow in a wet soil?

There is a long list of ground-cover plants that do well in a moist soil. Notice I said moist, not soupy wet. Too much water will restrict the growth of almost any plant.

Large, shrub-like plants do not do as well as the smaller, less conspicuous plants. The following ground-cover plants can do splendidly in soil that is moist for several months. Usually these conditions are found in the shade, so these plants also tolerate shady conditions.

Baby's-tears, bloodroot, bluets, coral bells, lily-turf, sand myrtle, and violets are just a few examples to aquaint you with the many different possibilities from which to choose.

383. What about foliar feeding of my ground-cover plants?

This will work fine so long as you supplement it at least once a year with a granular fertilizer. An occasional foliar feeding of the plants will stimulate them and keep them looking nicer throughout the growing season.

The fertilizer is absorbed through the leaves of the plant very rapidly and is quickly available to the plant. A sick-looking plant will benefit from this type of care. Don't worry about the water and fertilizer solution dripping to the ground. The nutrients will eventually work their way into the soil, where the roots will pick them up.

384. What insects do I need to be on the lookout for in my ground cover?

Fortunately, most ground-cover plants are not attacked by many insects. Just keep an eye on your plants so that in case a problem does develop you will become aware of it and solve it right away.

Scale insects, aphids, thrips, red spiders, lace bugs, and leafhoppers are a few of the more common insects you may encounter. Use an insecticide that is labeled for use on those insects you wish to kill. Handle these chemicals carefully and store them properly, out of the reach of small children.

385. I would like to plant ground cover on a slope beside my driveway. In the winter I'll have to shovel snow from the driveway onto the plants. Will this damage them in any way?

This will depend mostly on whether you use salt to keep the driveway free of ice. If you do, then you can expect problems with your ground-cover plants. Salt mixed in with the snow will accumulate in the ground-cover bed and will severely damage the plants.

You may select plants that are resistant to salt as one alternative to the problem, or buy calcium chloride instead of using a salt high in sodium. Calcium chloride is expensive, however.

386. My flowerbeds are very full of vigorously growing plants, most of which are dark green in color with a few flowers. Is there a ground cover I can use to add some color to my flowerbeds?

Yes. Choose a plant such as bloodroot, blue fescue, English lavender, or wooly thyme. Interspersed with the rest of your plants in the flowerbed, these ground covers will add a splash of silver coloring for you to enjoy.

Several other ground-cover plants may be used. Check with your local garden centers to see what is available in your area. Many of these plants can be seen in the spring seed catalogues and ordered by mail. Be sure to order your plants from a reputable company.

387. We have a country home where we spend the three summer months each year. We would like the place to look nice while we are there but be as maintenance-free as possible the rest of the year. Any suggestions?

You should avoid any types of plants that require year-round maintenance. Almost all of your perennial ground-cover plants fall into this category.

A good possibility for your particular needs might be an annual plant such as dwarf morning glory, sweet alyssum, or verbena. Seed them and they will form a carpet for the outdoor living area of your summer home. These plants will even reseed themselves for you.

After you have gone back to the city for the remainder of the year, these annual plants will thrive until the first frost nips them. The dead plants will decompose into the soil, making it richer for next year's plants.

388. What is the best way to clean trash and tree leaves from my ground-cover beds?

If you are talking about an occasional piece of paper or twigs blown by the wind, then just walk out into the bed and pick them up. When the debris is too much to pick up by hand, then use a fan rake, metal or bamboo.

These rakes are essential if you have any large trees that shed all their leaves onto your ground-cover bed. Leaves can smother the plants and cause a serious problem if you don't remove them. Experiment with one of these fan rakes and you'll soon learn how vigorously you can rake through the ground-cover plants without damaging them.

389. What are the names of some ground covers that will grow under the shade of an oak tree?

Five excellent ones for you to consider are English ivy, periwinkle, wintercreeper, pachistima, and Japanese spurge. All these plants will thrive in shade if you keep them fertilized and watered.

Out of the five plants listed, wintercreeper does the best under heavy shade conditions. It does equally well in full sun. Hardiness to cool temperatures and vigorous growth are two other main features of this ground cover. English ivy needs to be pruned occasionally to prevent it from becoming too tall. Baltic ivy is a lower-growing relative you may wish to use instead of the English ivy. Periwinkle has a nice, dark-green leaf and produces blue flowers on a trailing stem.

Pachistima is a fine-leafed evergreen that produces a red berry. This plant seldom grows more than 8 inches to 10 inches tall and is well suited to a shady location where a low-growing plant is needed. The Japanese spurge plant loves dense shade and soils with a high organic material in them.

Two other good shade-tolerant plants are the ornamental strawberry (*Fragaria chiloensis*) and carpet bugle.

390. Is dichondra a grass or a ground cover?

Dichondra is not a grass. It belongs to an entirely different group of plants than those found in the grass family, but it is an excellent ground-cover plant when given the proper care.

Usually you will find this plant thriving where the temperatures never drop below 20 degrees F. It does its best in southern California, southern Nevada, and in parts of Arizona. It has been estimated that in the Los Angeles area as much as 50 percent of the lawns are dichondra. It can be found in the majority of the other lawns as an unwanted guest. As a weed it is easy to remove from a grass lawn.

Dichondra withstands foot travel well when it is growing vigorously. To be at its best it needs to be mowed at about 1½ to 2 inches. It readily reseeds itself, which can be an advantage or a disadvantage, depending on whether you want it in your lawn or not.

391. Ferns grow abundantly in the woods near our home. Will these plants grow in my lawn?

It is difficult to give a clear-cut answer to this question. Usually the wild ferns can be dug up from their natural habitat and moved into gardens without too much difficulty. Be very careful not to damage the plant and dig up as much soil and roots as possible.

The plants need to be set in the same environment as that from which they were plucked. If they were in partial shade and moist soil, then you will have the best chance of their surviving by placing them in a similar spot in your garden.

If your soil is very different from that found in the woods, you may have some difficulties. Many plants do not survive when their roots are placed in a foreign soil.

When digging the plants in the woods, don't leave a mess behind. Disturb as little as possible. Fill in the holes when you get all the ferns you want. You don't want someone hiking in the woods to twist an ankle in a hole you left open.

392. Ferns always look so nice when found in the woods. How can I obtain enough of them to use as a ground cover?

These plants spread by an underground rootstock that may be divided to increase the number of plants available for planting. Many ferns have a crown that can be cut apart with a knife; these divisions will root quickly for you. A third method, which is more time-consuming, is to grow the ferns from spores (similar to seeds).

393. Is there a best time for transplanting ferns into my ground-cover beds?

These plants can be transplanted just about any time. Spring and fall transplantings, however, seem to give the best results. The key to being successful is in gentle handling. Avoid damaging the fronds (leaves) or breaking the soil away from the delicate roots.

Set the plants in the ground no deeper than they were before you dug them up. Add water and a little peat moss to the soil you pack around them.

394. What kind of flowering bulbs would grow best in my ground-cover beds?

You may choose from any number of a large variety of bulb plants. The type of ground cover you have will enter into your decision, along with your preference of flowers.

The following plants will give you some ideas, and you can easily add to this list without too much effort: crocus, galanthus, iris, narcissus, tuberous begonia, and tulips.

395. How well will my tulips and narcissus grow if I plant ground cover around them?

Both of these plants will do superbly in a ground-cover bed. They add a touch of color to the area and offer a contrasting texture to give the bed added interest.

As summer draws nearer the tulips and narcissus become very unattractive as the leaves shrivel up and die, but when growing in with the ground cover plants the yellowing leaves are less noticeable. They seem to get lost in the overall beauty of the rest of the plants.

396. I have a lot of unattractive, exposed areas in my ground-cover beds. What should I do?

First, if you have a vine-like or creeping ground cover, try laying some of the longer vines or stems over into the bare spots. Before long they will have branched out and filled in these unsightly spots for you.

You can replant some of the plants from an overcrowded spot into the bare area. Don't forget ground covers are adapted to fill in quickly, especially if watered and fertilized.

397. Would a ground cover be practical growing between the cracks in flagstones on my garden path?

Several tough little plants are available and practical for this job. Some are even fragrant when stepped on, giving a pleasant scent to your garden as you take an evening stroll. You may choose between shade- and sun-loving plants, depending upon where your garden path leads to.

Chapter 16 has a list of the ground covers that do well growing in the cracks of flagstones and rocks. These types of ground covers are often referred to as paving plants.

398. My neighbor is always bragging about how nice her English ivy grows in the shade. When I correct her and tell her she has Baltic ivy, she insists I am wrong. What is the proper name for this plant?

You both are probably correct. English and Baltic ivy closely resemble each other. Both do well in the shade, and if you go by leaf shape to identify them, you will have a difficult time.

Baltic ivy is a little more cold-hardy and grows lower to the ground than does English ivy. If you want a good, shade-tolerant ground cover, which is long lived, choose English ivy. It is probably one of the most popular of the ground covers throughout the United States and overseas.

399. My ajuga (carpet bugle) was looking really nice until the hot summer months. Then the variegated leaves began turning brown and dying. What is happening to my plants?

Any of a large number of problems could have beset your plants. Two good possibilities are leaf burn and droughty conditions.

If the plants looked healthy and were doing well in the spring and then the leaves turned brown in the summer, it is likely the hotter sun rays actually burned the delicate leaves. The ground covers with variegated leaves should always be planted in a shady spot where they are protected from the sun.

Lack of sufficient water will also cause the leaves to turn brown and die. Carpet bugle is a shallow-rooted plant and therefore needs to be watered regularly. Keeping the soil moist could solve your problem and make your plants more vigorous and healthy looking.

Appendix A

TEMPERATURE CONVERSION GUIDE

Fahrenheit   Celsius

(F)   (C)

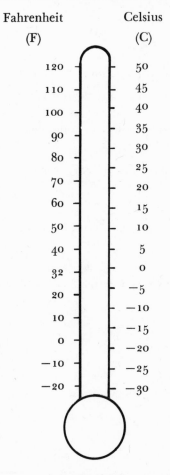

Fahrenheit (F)	Celsius (C)
120	50
110	45
100	40
90	35
80	30
	25
70	20
60	15
50	10
40	5
32	0
20	−5
	−10
10	−15
0	−20
−10	−25
−20	−30

When converting temperatures you need to know these two formulas:

$$C = \frac{5}{9}(F - 32) \quad \text{and} \quad F = \frac{9\,(C)}{5} + 32$$

Follow the conversion of two different temperatures to see how these formulas work.

EXAMPLE: Change 10 degrees Celsius to Fahrenheit

$$\text{Step 1} \quad F = \frac{9 \times 10}{5} + 32$$

$$\text{Step 2} \quad F = \frac{90}{5} + 32$$

$$\text{Step 3} \quad F = 18 + 32$$

$$\text{Step 4} \quad F = 50 \text{ degrees Fahrenheit}$$

EXAMPLE: Change 212 degrees Fahrenheit to Celsius

$$\text{Step 1} \quad C = \frac{5}{9}(212 - 32)$$

$$\text{Step 2} \quad C = \frac{5}{9}(180)$$

$$\text{Step 3} \quad C = \frac{900}{9}$$

$$\text{Step 4} \quad C = 100 \text{ degrees Celsius}$$

Appendix B

STANDARD U.S. MEASURES

Liquid

1 ounce	=	2 tablespoons
1 tablespoon	=	3 teaspoons
1 cup	=	16 tablespoons
2 cups	=	1 pint
16 ounces	=	1 pint
2 pints	=	1 quart
4 quarts	=	1 gallon

Linear

12 inches	=	1 foot
3 feet	=	1 yard
1,760 yards	=	1 mile
5,280 feet	=	1 mile

Square

144 sq. in.	=	1 sq. ft.
9 sq. ft	=	1 sq. yd.
43,560 sq. ft.	=	1 sq. acre
1,000 sq. ft.	=	$\frac{1}{43}$ sq. acre

Appendix C

WEIGHTS AND MEASURES

ENGLISH (U.S.) SYSTEM   METRIC EQUIVALENCE

Dry Weight

1 ounce	=	28.35	grams
1 pound	=	435.59	grams
1 ton	=	907.18	kilograms

Liquid Measurements

1 ounce	=	29.575	milliliters
1 pint	=	0.4732	liters
1 quart	=	0.9463	liters
1 gallon	=	3.7850	liters

Linear Measurements

1 inch	=	2.54	centimeters
1 foot	=	0.3048	meters
1 yard	=	0.9144	meters
1 mile	=	1.6093	meters

Square Measurements

1 square inch	=	6.452	square centimeters
1 square foot	=	929.0	square centimeters
1 square yard	=	0.836	square meters
100 square feet	=	9.29	square meters
1,000 square feet	=	92.9	square meters

WEIGHTS AND MEASURES

METRIC SYSTEM	APPROXIMATE U.S. EQUIVALENCE

Dry Weight

1 gram	=	0.035 ounces
1 kilogram	=	2.2 pounds
1 metric ton	=	1.1 English tons

Liquid Measurements

29.5 milliliters	=	1.0 ounce
1 liter	=	1.06 quarts

Linear Measurements

1 millimeter	=	0.04 inches
1 centimeter	=	0.39 inches
1 meter	=	39.37 inches
1 kilometer	=	0.62 miles

Square Measurements

1 square centimeter	=	0.155 square inches
1 square meter	=	1.2 square yards

Glossary

Aerification	process of mechanically punching holes through the grass and thatch, removing small plugs of soil which allows better air and water movement in the soil.
Balanced fertilizer	any fertilizer material which has the major nutrients (nitrogen, phosphorus, and potassium) in proportions best suited to grass plant needs.
Blend	a mixture of two or more types of grass seed of the same species.
Broad spectrum pesticide	any chemical that is capable of killing a wide range of bothersome pests.
Bunch grass	any grass that does not develop rhizomes and stolons.
Carrier	inert filler used to absorb plant nutrients so as to allow even distribution of nutrients throughout the fertilizer material.
Colorant	a liquid dye, usually green, sprayed on plants to improve their appearance, most commonly used on brown dormant grass plants during the winter months.
Complete fertilizer	any fertilizer material that contains the three major plant nutrients—nitrogen, phosphorus, and potassium.
Cotyledon	seedling leaves that first emerge from the seed.
Creeping grass	any grass that spreads by means of underground rhizomes or aboveground stolons.
Crown	growing point of a grass plant, located at the base of the plant just above the soil level.
Cyclone spreader	mechanical spreader which spreads fertilizer or seed out parallel to the ground in a fan shape.
Dethatch	removal of thatch from a lawn, either manually with a rake or by gasoline-powered equipment.

Dormant	a resting period which plants enter when placed under stress; growth ceases during the stress periods.
Dormant seed	seed that is in a resting stage, awaiting proper conditions to begin the germination process.
Dwarf grass	refers to the growth patterns of the newer grass varieties. Individual leaves of the grass plant grow out at an angle from the plant rather than straight upward. Allows the grass to be mowed shorter.
Environment	all external factors that influence the growth of any plants or animals.
Farm-type fertilizer	plant food which is very water soluble; nitrogen usually in ammonium and nitrate forms; burns plant parts readily if misapplied.
Fertilizer	any material containing plant food.
Fertilizer burn	damage suffered by a plant when a dry commercial fertilizer is applied to a wet plant. Salt from the fertilizer draws moisture from the plant's cells, killing it or causing brown spots on the leaves.
Fruiting bodies	reproductive centers in fungi where seed-like structures are formed.
Fungicide	any chemical used to kill fungi.
Fungus	a parasitic form of plant life that is incapable of manufacturing its own food due to the lack of chlorophyll in any of its own cells.
Germination	process of dormant seed changing to an emerging seedling.
Grade	refers to the percent of nitrogen, phosphorus, and potassium present in a fertilizer.
Ground covers	any plant used to cover an area to prevent soil erosion, conserve soil moisture or for aesthetic reasons.
Growth retardants	chemicals sprayed on plants to slow down or stop their growth altogether.
Herbicide	any chemical compound used to kill plants.
Insecticide	any chemical used for killing insects.
Lateral buds	growing points of plants found along the sides of the main stem; cause side shoots to develop.
Lime	any material used to raise the pH of an acid soil to a more favorable reading for good plant growth.
Major nutrients	those plant nutrients needed in large amounts to sustain the plant's growth.
Manicure	to perform extra lawn-care practices to improve the overall appearance of your lawn.

Micro-climate	the actual growing conditions around the grass plant; usually from 0 to 4 inches above the soil surface.
Micro-organisms	minute creatures such as bacteria, protozoa, actinomycetes which live in the soil; invisible to the naked eye.
Minor nutrients	those plant nutrients needed in small amounts by plants, but absolutely necessary to their health.
Mulch	any material spread out in a layer over the soil surface; may be used to prevent soil erosion, conserve soil moisture or as decorative ground cover.
Nematode	microscopic, worm-like animals that can cause serious injury to plants.
Overseeding	spreading seed over an area which already has some sort of plant cover; usually a thin, worn-out grass area.
Pesticide	any chemical used to kill pests (insects, fungi, weeds, nematodes, mites, etc.).
pH	scientific designation used to show whether a soil is acid (high in hydrogen) or alkaline. A pH of 7 is neutral, higher than 7 is alkaline and lower is acid.
Photosynthesis	production of food in green plants due to the chemical reaction between light and the water and carbon dioxide contained in the plant cells.
Plugs	cylindrical cores of sod removed from a lawn; used for starting new lawns and repairing bare spots.
Postemergent chemicals	any substances which when sprayed on living plants kills or seriously retards their growth.
Preemergent chemicals	any substances applied onto the soil that prevent seeds from germinating and seedlings from maturing.
Propagation	the process of increasing plant populations through the use of seed, cuttings, plugs, sprigs, sod, or division.
Ratio	the proportion of nitrogen, phosphorus, and potassium to each other in a fertilizer; a 30-10-20 has a ratio of 3:1:2.
Renovation	to improve or repair an existing lawn without tearing it up.
Rhizome	an underground stem which grows parallel to, but just below, the soil surface. New plants shoot up from this structure, allowing bare spots in a lawn to quickly fill in with grass plants.
Rootstock	an underground root-like stem; see rhizome.

Rootzone	soil where the plant roots grow.
Scalping	mowing the grass too short, usually cutting it off just above ground level; frequently removing the crown of the grass and severely damaging the plant.
Saline	refers to a soil that has a very high quantity of sodium in it.
Seedbed	an area of prepared soil which is ready for seeding.
Shelf life	length of time pesticides can be stored before they lose their effectiveness.
Soil reservoir	microscopic pockets in the soil where air, water, and nutrients are held for plant use.
Soil sterilant	chemicals used to kill all living organisms in the soil; useful in getting rid of bothersome pests often found in the soil.
Soil texture	a property of the soil determined by the percentages of sand, silt, and clay present in it.
Soluble salts	salts contained within a fertilizer which are readily dissolved when water comes into contact with the fertilizer material.
Sprigs	pieces of the grass plant that are used to start new lawns; stolons (runners) are present in these pieces.
Starter fertilizer	any fertilizer material that is low in nitrogen but high in phosphorus and potassium; used on newly seeded lawns to supply the plants with the specific nutrients needed for rapid and strong growth.
Stolon	an aboveground stem that runs along the soil surface; rooting occurs and new plants develop from these runners. Sprigs are pieces of stolons.
Systemic pesticide	any chemical that is absorbed by the roots and moves·throughout the plant, giving it internal protection against any attacking pests.
Thatch	an accumulated layer of dead and decaying grass stems and leaves located just above the soil surface.
Tillering	new plants that develop from around the base of the mature grass plant.
Topdressing	a specially prepared mixture of soil, spread over a lawn to improve it by filling in low spots and reducing thatch.
Variegated leaves	leaves displaying two or more colors.
Variety	group of plants which are very similar in many characteristics; a sub-grouping below the species level in the plant naming system.
Weed	any plant growing where it is not wanted.

Index